59ML

1/4 CUP = 59ML
1/3 CUP = 79ML
1/2 CUP = 118ML
1 CUP = 237ML

1/8 TSP = 0.63ML
1/4 TSP = 1.25ML
1/2 TSP = 2.5ML
3/4 TSP = 3.75ML
1 TSP = 5ML
1 TBSP = 15ML

1 INCH = 2.54CM

32°F = 0°C
320°F = 160°C
375°F = 190°C

118ML

237ML

IF YOU CAN'T
SAY IT
WITH WORDS,
SAY IT WITH
CHICKEN

IF YOU CAN'T SAY IT WITH WORDS, SAY IT WITH CHICKEN

Gabriele Edlbauer & *Julia* S. Goodman

To *all the chickens in the world.*

Table of Contents

Before You Begin

Introduction 9

Notes on Measuring, Kosher Salt & Salmonella 11

Schmaltz & Gribenes 14

Recipes

We're Too Entangled Chicken
Chicken Liver Pasta 16

I'm a Smoker Chicken
Chicken Nuggets with Two Dips
& Chicken Fat Washed Bourbon Cocktail 22

You've Changed Chicken
Russian Chicken 28

Let's Just Be Friends Chicken
Caesar Salad 34

I Want to Move in Chicken
Chicken Pot Pie 40

Let's Take Things Slow Chicken
Sous Vide Chicken Breast with Fried Skin & Mole 46

I Left the Church Chicken
Pope's Nose Amuse-bouche 52

I've Had a Change of Heart Chicken
Chicken-filled Coconut Macaroons 56

You Were Our Backup Plan Chicken
Basic Roast Chicken 64

I'm Very Sick Chicken
Matzo Ball Soup 70

I Love You Chicken
Brined Roast Chicken with Tomatoes 76

I Froze My Eggs Chicken
Chicken Sorbet & Egg, Turmeric, Cardamom Ice Cream 82

Let's Be Friends with Benefits Chicken
Backhendl Salat 88

I Hate You Chicken
Salmonella Spell 94

Meet My Parents Chicken
Deviled Eggs & Chopped Liver 100

Give Me a Second Chance Chicken
Sloppy Chicken Sandwiches 106

I'm Not the Person You Think I Am Chicken
Currywurst Chicken-filled French Fries with Reversed Ketchup & Mayo 112

Goodbye Chicken
Babka Chicken Salad Sandwiches 120

Information

About 129

We Would Like to Thank 131

Credits 133

Imprint 135

If You Can't Say It with Words, Say It with Chicken

Introduction
by Gabriele Edlbauer & Julia S. Goodman

Most of the important memories in Julia's life involve chicken: mustard chicken, apricot chicken, roast chicken, schmaltz with onions, chopped chicken livers on challah bread, and of course the queen of all chicken dishes, matzo ball soup. Since her family always has a fitting chicken recipe at hand for all holidays, including weekly Shabbat dinners, it was only natural that the bird would become Julia's delicious go-to accomplice. All of her memories of chicken are good, even when they are bad, like when she got whooping cough at age 10 from sharing chicken fingers with her best friend, they still were worth it! Julia's family roots stem from predominantly Eastern European Jews who emigrated to the USA in the early 20th century. This culinary heritage is a huge part of why Julia calls herself a proud Jewish American Princess – even though this term leaves a derogatory aftertaste.

While there certainly are plenty of chicken dishes where Gabi grew up on an organic farm in the predominantly Catholic Mühlviertel in Upper Austria, her most distinct chicken-y childhood memories are less culinarily associated. They involve the sale of eggs with her mom, chasing after free-range chickens at the family farm and a nasty oral infection after eating chicken poop when she was 4.

And so while Julia's connection to the bird started at the supermarket and ended at the dinner table, Gabi's was more integrated into a larger economic system of the household and farm. Through sharing these stories we realized how oddly similar our relationships to chicken are to our artistic approaches. While creating narratives is typically at the center of both our individual and joint artistic practices, our strategies are quite different. Gabi humorously challenges structural or political relationships while Julia often relies on memory-heavy emotional realities.

Julia's chicken obsession moved to Austria with her and Gabi was here for it. Chicken quickly became a shopping list staple and the center of almost all dinners ever hosted in our household. With chicken present at so many intimate occasions, one obsession led to another as we began to question how certain dishes have the power to convey or trigger very specific feelings.

Inspired by famed US-American cookbook author and TV-personality Ina Garten's roast chicken recipe, we had the desire to further address this phenomenon by combining our chicken enthusiasm with our artistic experience. With her dish, now famously called 'engagement chicken', Ina Garten sparked a long series of marriage proposals.

It became glaringly obvious to us that chicken can resolve more than the question of matrimony. While not all feelings are equally hard to address for everyone, with this book we wanted to create recipes that focus on supporting anyone who's preoccupied with the sometimes-difficult task of finding the right words.

Whenever you need it, chicken can help you set boundaries, make commitments and admit the cold, hard truths. The photos in the book are there to display our artistic serving suggestions for the emotionally charged dishes. But, no matter what your plates or cutlery, the food's message should still ring clear in your kitchen. It doesn't have to be all on you! Let the chicken do the talking.

Notes on Measuring, Kosher Salt & Salmonella

Measuring

Online, as well as in our friendship circles, there is a passionate argument about who is right and who is wrong with *their* way of measuring out ingredients for a recipe. Which system is more exact? What is more practical and mathematically doable while cooking? And why haven't the US, Myanmar and Liberia ever joined the metric system?

Lovers of the scale tend to degrade volumetric cup measurements as inexact, but let's be real here: malfunctioning scales have also been at the epicenter of many baking catastrophes. While metric math stands for the idea of being more logical, in the heat of the moment, any way of calculating can fail. So, one can only conclude that no matter how *you* personally approach the delicate subject of measuring, it will be right for *somebody*.

In this book we tried to give the reader a few paths towards the right amounts. Sometimes (especially when measuring out spices) this led us to rather ridiculous numbers. Other times, specifically with the ice cream recipe, there is no way around a precision scale. While almost always both volumetric and weight amounts appear, if you choose to work with cup and spoon measurements, please keep the following in mind:

* The cup size we're using throughout this book is the standardized US dry measuring cup which contains 236.588 ml. If you aren't sure if the cup in your kitchen is the right volume, please double check.

* The tablespoon size lands at 14.7868 ml (or ½ oz) and the teaspoon at 4.9289 ml (or 1/6 oz).

For your weighing pleasure, when calculating the metric conversions we took the liberty to round these measurements up or down to beautiful, less outlandish numbers – you won't even taste the difference.

Salt, or What the Hell Is Kosher Salt?

Since so many recipes in this cookbook are embracing Julia's Jewish heritage, the choice for using kosher salt was always *crystal* clear. Kosher salt is very popular among chefs since it has wider, coarser grains than those of table salt and a lower salinity per volume. This makes it easy and satisfying to season food with your fingers and therefore hard to oversalt. Unlike common table salt, kosher salt's flakier texture dissolves on and sticks to food perfectly. US-American households have adopted this ingredient as a staple, but when Julia came to Austria she sadly discovered her only option was to import it in her suitcase.

Contrary to what one would imagine when first reading the term kosher salt, there isn't a rabbi blessing every box leaving the factory. While there have been, and still are religious connections (the salt is named after the process of koshering meat), the product as it's sold today goes far beyond Jewish culinary traditions.

When it comes to grain size and salinity by volume, not all brands of kosher salt are equal. We use Diamond Crystal Kosher Salt in our home and throughout this cookbook. Do not worry if this brand or kind of salt is difficult to source in your country, below is a simple chart to help you out.

Weight of 1 Tablespoon:

Table Salt	19 grams
Fine Sea Salt	15 grams
Morton Kosher Salt	15 grams
Sel Gris (Unrefined French Sea Salt)	13 grams
Diamond Crystal Kosher Salt	10 grams

Raw chicken – oh how the sight of those two words together has the ability to cause dread and worry among the most confident home cooks. Do not panic! Basic kitchen cleanliness and techniques should help avoid any stomachaches.

Firstly, the old tradition of washing your chicken is totally outdated. Actually, if you take one lesson away from this book let this be it! Unless you are killing and butchering the bird yourself, there really should be no need for the rinsing off process. In fact, in washing the bird you are producing a higher risk of illness by spreading the bacteria and raw chicken juices around your kitchen sink. Plus, by unnecessarily wetting the bird you can affect browning later.

Secondly, feel very welcome to set aside one of your non-porous cutting boards for the sole purpose of cutting and seasoning raw meat. This is optional but helpful for keeping an overview of chicken-contaminated surfaces.

Thirdly, be sure to avoid contaminating other surfaces around the kitchen by diligently cleaning those that have come in contact with the raw bird. This should include the countertop area under the cutting board, your knives and sink.

And, finally, when seasoning a whole chicken, we like to pre-measure some salt in a bowl. That way there is no need to contaminate your precious kosher salt jar. Plan for around 1 tsp (3 g) of kosher salt per 1 lb (0.45 kg) of meat.

Schmaltz & Gribenes

Rendered Chicken
Fat & Crispy
Skin

2 ¼ lb (1 kg)
chicken skin,
partially frozen[1]
1 ½ tsp (4.5 g)
kosher salt
½ tsp (1.5 g)
freshly ground
black pepper
2 medium yellow
onions, cut in
¼ in (0.5 cm)
thick slices

1.
Start by cutting your chicken skin into small ½ in (1-2 cm) pieces.[2]

2.
Over a stove on medium-low heat, add your chicken skin pieces, salt and pepper to a Dutch oven or large nonstick skillet with a lid. Stir the seasonings to coat the skin and cover for 15 minutes.

3.
Remove the lid from your pan, by this time some liquid fat will have started to appear. Give everything a stir and turn the heat up to medium. Cook, stirring regularly for about 5 minutes before adding the sliced onions.

4.
Cook for another 30 minutes or so, first to soften the onions and then to begin browning the skin. Stir frequently, turning down the heat if the browning starts to become uneven.

5.
Remove your pan from the heat and pour the skin, onions and schmaltz through a metal strainer that is set over a heat-proof bowl.

6.
Leave the fat in the bowl and return the onion and chicken skin mixture to the skillet, setting the stove to medium heat. Cook, stirring regularly, to finish rendering any fat and crisping the skin, which when finished should be deeply golden brown.

7.
Using a slotted spoon or tongs, move the chicken skin and onions onto a paper towel to rid them of any excess oil, season straight away with a light sprinkling of salt. These are now finished and ready to be eaten![3]

8.
Any precious fat left in the bottom of the pan after removing the skin can also be strained and added to the rest of the schmaltz you rendered earlier.

9.
Once all of the fat has rendered, pour it into a heat-proof, non-reactive container and bring to room temperature before storing it in the fridge.[4]

1 It's a little tricky to offer exact portion sizes for this recipe since it varies depending on how fatty the skins are. That being said, 2 ¼ lb (1 kg) of chicken skin should amount to about 1 ½ cups (360 ml) of rendered chicken fat.

2 The chicken skin does not need to be frozen but it is significantly easier to cut into small pieces if it is. Our favorite way is to leave it in the freezer overnight and then (using a serrated knife or chef's knife) cut the larger block into smaller strips and then cut the strips into small bite-size pieces. If you want to skip this step, a pair of kitchen scissors works well if the skin is just out of the fridge.

3 These are also used as a seasoning for the deviled eggs in *Meet My Parents Chicken* on page 100.

4 Your schmaltz will be good for about a month if stored well (as suggested above) in the fridge.

We’re Too Entangled

Chicken

We're Too Entangled Chicken

Chicken Liver Pasta

When your overly-enthusiastic therapist signs up for that yoga class you're teaching, when you realize the nagging child you used to babysit is now your boss, or when your parents still want to be friends with your ex...you have every right to feel exposed, bewildered and overwhelmed. If you don't want every aspect of your life to mix together, set some boundaries with this pasta.

However confusing the list of ingredients may seem, they come together to form a dish with an intense, balanced and luxurious clarity;[1] much like the outcome you hope to acquire from cooking it for the person sitting across the table.

Makes 4~6 servings

For the Sauce

2 small shallots, diced
3 garlic cloves, roughly chopped
⅔ lb (300 g) chicken livers, cut into bite-sized pieces
2 tbs (30 ml) olive oil
2 tbs (30 ml) mirin
¼ cup (60 ml) cognac
2 cups (480 ml) beef stock
2 cups (480 ml) chicken stock
1 sprig of rosemary
freshly ground black pepper
½ tsp (1.5 g) kosher salt
1 tbs + 1 tsp (30 g) red miso
3 tbs (42 g) cold butter, cut into small pieces
1 package (500 g) squid ink pasta

For the Breadcrumb Topping

3 tbs (45 ml) olive oil
1 sprig of rosemary
¾ cup (40 g) panko
¼ cup (15 g) pecorino, finely grated
zest of 1 lemon
¼ tsp (a big pinch) red chili flakes

1.

Start your sauce by cleaning and patting dry the chicken livers, cutting off any stringy bits. Heat your olive oil in a shallow pot on medium-high and fry the livers until brown on both sides.[2] Move to a plate and set aside. Don't worry too much about overcooking the livers since they will be puréed later in the recipe.

2.

Now add your chopped shallots into the remaining olive oil and liver fat coated pan, cook for 4–5 minutes until translucent and just starting to brown. Be sure the heat isn't too high.

3.

Add the garlic and cook for another minute or so, until fragrant.

4.

Deglaze the pan with Cognac, scraping up any bits at the bottom. Let the liquor simmer for about 2 minutes until it has reduced by half.

5.

Add your mirin, stock, rosemary sprig (whole), chicken livers, salt and pepper to the pan. Bring to a simmer and turn heat to low so it can bubble very gently for about 15–20 minutes, partially covered with a lid.

6.

This is a good time to **prepare the breadcrumbs**. In a small sauté pan, start by heating 3 tbs (45 ml) of olive oil along with one sprig of rosemary. Let the rosemary gently fry in the oil, until crisp but not burned, on both sides. Remove to a paper towel with tongs and season with a pinch of salt. This step helps drain the excess oil from the herbs for later on.

7.

Now, to your fragrant oil, add the panko and a generous pinch of salt and pepper. Mix with a spatula to coat all of the breadcrumbs with the oil and stir constantly to toast the breadcrumbs. This will happen fast so keep stirring until they are nicely golden brown.

8.

Remove the breadcrumbs to a bowl and mix with the grated pecorino, lemon zest and chili flakes. Stir to get the pecorino evenly distributed. The cheese will start to melt slightly, resulting in something delicious where the cheese and the breadcrumbs form little clusters.

9.

With your fingers, pull the fried rosemary leaves from the woody stem and crumble them into the breadcrumbs. Stir. This is your topping.

10.

After the livers have simmered with the other ingredients for about 20 minutes, remove from the heat. Pick out the rosemary sprig with tongs and half of the livers and discard.

11.

Pour the remaining half of the livers along with the shallot, garlic and cooking liquid into a blender. You likely need to do this in batches as the mixture is hot! Purée carefully until very smooth.

12.

Wipe out the same shallow pot you used earlier and pour contents from the blender through a large fine-mesh strainer back into the pot.

13.

If the mixture is very liquidy, simmer until slightly reduced. You want it to be a similar consistency to buttermilk. Be mindful not to over-reduce as you will cook the pasta in the sauce and it will thicken further.

14.

Over low heat, once the sauce is warmed again, whisk in the cold butter, 1 small piece at a time. This helps to emulsify the butter into the sauce. After the butter is fully incorporated, whisk in the miso.

15.

Taste and season if need be with salt or more pepper. Turn off the heat.

16.

Boil your pasta in very salty water.

17.

About 2–3 minutes before the pasta is finished cooking, put the sauce back on the heat. Drain your spaghetti and add it to your pot with the sauce, reserving some pasta-cooking water. Simmer together, adding a bit of pasta water if the sauce is too thick. Keep stirring over medium-low heat until the pasta is finished cooking and is nicely coated by the sauce. The sauce will continue to thicken after plating, so be mindful to keep it on the looser side.

18.

Serve in a pasta bowl topped with a few spoonfuls of your breadcrumb mixture.

1 This dish is very decadent. It's great with a very acidic, herby salad or could be a small starter.

2 For cooking, we like using a wide, low-sided 4.4 qts (4.3 l) pot for this, it should also have a lid.

I’m a Smoker Chicken

I'm a Smoker Chicken
Chicken Nuggets with Two Dips & Chicken Fat Washed Bourbon Cocktail

Makes 25 Nuggets & 1 Cocktail

Chicken Nuggets

For the Nugget Mixture
2 ¼ lb (1 kg) ground chicken thighs
2 ½ tsp (8 g) kosher salt
1 tsp (2.5 g) ground white pepper
1 tsp (4 g) MSG
1 ½ tsp (4.5 g) smoked paprika
1 ½ tsp (4.5 g) Kashmiri chili powder
1 ½ tsp (4.5 g) onion powder
1 ½ tsp (6 g) garlic powder
¼ tsp (a big pinch) freshly ground black pepper

For the Honey Mustard Sauce
¼ cup (55 g) mayonnaise
2 tbs (34 g) Dijon mustard
2 tbs (30 ml) honey
1 tsp (3 g) mustard powder
1 tbs (15 ml) apple cider vinegar
¼ tsp (a big pinch) of kosher salt
½ tsp (2.5 ml) fish sauce

For the Herb Sauce
2 cups (100 g) coriander + stems
1 ½ cups (75 g) parsley + stems
2 cloves garlic
2 tbs (30 ml) lemon juice
1 ½ tsp (4.5 g) kosher salt
¼ cup (60 ml) water (or more if needed)
1 tbs (15 ml) agave syrup

For the Dry Dredge
3 cups (370 g) cornstarch
⅔ cup (100 g) potato starch
⅔ cup (80 g) AP flour
2 ½ tsp (8 g) kosher salt
1 tsp (2.5 g) ground white pepper
1 ½ tsp (4.5 g) smoked paprika
1 ½ tsp (4.5 g) Kashmiri chili powder
1 ½ tsp (4.5 g) onion powder
1 ½ tsp (6 g) garlic powder
¼ tsp (a big pinch) of freshly ground black pepper

For the Wet Dredge
4 eggs
½ cup (120 ml) buttermilk

For Frying
vegetable oil[1]

Cocktail

For the Fat Washed Bourbon
12 ½ oz (375 ml) bourbon, high proof[2]
1 oz (30 ml) chicken schmaltz[3]

For the Smoking Cocktail
2 oz (60 ml) chicken fat washed bourbon
¾ oz (22.5 ml) 3:1 honey syrup
¾ oz (22.5 ml) fresh lemon juice
1 ½ oz (45 ml) fresh yellow bell pepper juice[4]
hickory wood chips for cold smoker

1 You will be deep frying, so be sure to have a large bottle of neutral flavored oil with a high smoking temperature. This includes e.g. sunflower, corn, peanut, etc.
2 We use Wild Turkey Rare Breed.
3 See page 14.
4 This can be done in a juicer or blender. Just be sure to remove the stems and seeds and strain out any solids with a fine-mesh strainer or nut-milk bag before using.

If you smoke, it's likely that there is someone in your life who disapproves. Concealing your cigarettes or other smoking-related items might seem like an easy fix to avoid confrontation but will get even more challenging as you become closer. Accidental slip-ups, such as the noticeable smell of smoke on your clothes or a photo shared by a friend, may inadvertently unveil your status. As an admission and an acceptance of your habit, prepare this pairing to face your truth.

Smoking, in cooking, might be less controversial and perhaps one of the most historical flavors. Triggering many senses and memories, it's no question that smoky food and drinks have a particularly special allure. Helpfully, this recipe spills the secret for you by associating itself with your habit, allowing for an easier entry into this ultimately difficult conversation.

1.
Start by grinding the chicken thighs with a meat grinder or food processor.

2.
Measure and mix all the nugget mixture spices for the 'marinade'.

3.
Add the spice mix to a large bowl with the ground chicken and, wearing disposable gloves, mix by hand. Cover and let it sit overnight in the fridge, or for at least 1 hour.

4.
The next day, again wearing gloves, form the chicken mixture into about 25 small, nugget shaped pieces and place flat on a baking-paper lined sheet tray.[5]

5.
Refrigerate again, for at least 30 minutes.

6.
Now is a good time to **work on your 2 dipping sauces.** For the honey mustard sauce, add all ingredients into a small bowl, whisk until combined and set aside.

7.
For the herb sauce, place all ingredients into your blender and purée until smooth. Pour into another small bowl and set aside.

8.
Prepare your 2 dredges. In a large bowl, mix the dry dredge ingredients. Whisk until incorporated. Split the mixture evenly into 2 shallow dishes.

9.
In a medium sized bowl, whisk the eggs and buttermilk until combined.

10.
Prepare another baking tray lined with baking paper.

11.
For the dredging process, start by dipping each nugget, one at a time, first into the dry mixture, then the wet, and again into the second tray of the dry. Make sure to really pack on the final dry coating. Shake off any excess and lay your nuggets, in a single layer, on your prepared baking tray. Refrigerate the fully dredged nuggets for about 7 minutes in the fridge. This helps the dredge to adhere to the meat.

12.
On your stove, fill a large heavy bottomed pot halfway with your neutral flavored oil and attach a suitable thermometer.[6] Bring to 350°F (180°C).

13.
Carefully place the nuggets into the oil one at a time, until there are a few in your pot. Avoid overcrowding. With a spider or slotted spoon, every so often, gently move them around to be sure they don't stick to one another. Fry for 6–7 minutes and remove, placing them onto a wire rack. Repeat with your remaining nuggets, in batches, always being sure that your oil has come back to the correct temperature before adding more.

14.
Once all of the nuggets have been fried, bring your oil back to 350°F (180°C) and fry again. This second fry is really just to be sure the outside is nice and crisp, so fry for only about 2–3 minutes, in batches as before and place on a wire rack once done.

15.
Immediately season lightly with salt and serve with your two sauces on the side.

5 To prevent sticking it helps to have a small bowl of water to occasionally wet your hands with as you form the nuggets.
6 Do not fill the pot more than halfway as the oil will expand when hot.

Cocktail

1.

For your fat washed bourbon, warm up chicken schmaltz in a small saucepan or microwave until just melted.

2.

To a mason jar or non-reactive container, add your bourbon and the schmaltz. Stir.

3.

Close the container and infuse for 4 hours at room temperature. Agitate the container by shaking every 30 minutes.[7]

4.

Put the jar into your freezer until the fat has separated and is frozen solid.

5.

Take your container out of the freezer and immediately strain the contents through a fine-mesh strainer to remove the fat. Discard fat. You should be left with clear schmaltz-tasting bourbon.[8]

6.

Now it's time to make your cocktail. Combine your bourbon, honey syrup, lemon juice and fresh yellow bell pepper juice in a cocktail shaker filled with ice.

7.

Shake vigorously for 8–10 seconds. Double strain over fresh ice into a double-old fashioned glass.

8.

Cover and cold smoke the cocktail with hickory wood chips.[9] Uncover when serving to release the smoke and aromas.

7 The purpose of this is to be sure that the fat doesn't solidify into one clump (at this point) and is consistently mixing and in contact with the liquor.

8 If there are any small fat particles left, you can pass the bourbon through a coffee filter for a second strain.

9 To cold smoke our cocktail, we use The Smoking Gun by Sage.

You've Changed Chicken

Makes 6–8 servings

FOR Russian dressing

scant 3 cups (690 g) ketchup (preferably Heinz)
2 tbs-¼ cup (30–50 g) granulated sugar (to taste)
¼ cup (60 ml) water (more if too thick)
¼ cup (60 ml) vegetable oil
3 tbs (45 ml) fresh lemon juice
1 tbs (15 ml) vinegar (apple cider or white wine)
1 ½ tsp (2.5 g) celery seeds[1]
2 tbs (30 ml) Worcestershire sauce (more to taste)
¼ cup (60 g) grated onion

1. Preheat your oven to 330°F (165°C).
2. Start by adding all of the RUSSIAN DRESSING ingredients together in a large mixing bowl. Whisk, by hand, to combine.

FOR Chicken preparation

4 bone-in, skin-on chicken breasts, cut in half[2]
4 bone-in, skin-on chicken thighs
4 bone-in, skin-on chicken legs
2 × 1.4 oz (40 g) packages dry onion soup mix
2 × 13 oz (370 g) jars apricot jam[3]
1 or 2 splashes of dry vermouth

3. Add both jars of apricot jam, both packages of onion soup mix and your vermouth to the bowl with the Russian dressing. Whisk by hand to combine.
4. PLACE ALL OF THE CHICKEN PIECES into a large glass oven-safe dish with high sides.
5. Pour your sauce all over the chicken and cover the dish with aluminum foil.[4]
6. Place the baking dish in the center of the oven for about 1–1 ½ hours until the chicken has cooked all the way through.
7. When done, carefully remove your dish from the oven. Let it cool before putting it in the refrigerator overnight.[5]
8. THE NEXT DAY, remove the chicken from the refrigerator, uncover and discard the aluminum foil. Let it sit on your countertop for about 30–45 minutes so it gets closer to room temperature.
9. PREHEAT THE OVEN to 375°F (190°C). Place your chicken, still uncovered, near the middle or top of your oven for about 20 minutes or until the sauce has thickened and the chicken is warmed through and nicely browned.

You've Changed Chicken

Russian Chicken

In the case of most of the dishes in this book, their preparation methods and presentations are intended to go hand in hand with their emotional pairings. In this instance, the chicken not only makes you grapple with change, but has been subjected to it itself.

Russian chicken has been served in Julia's family for a long time. It is a classic on Rosh Hashanah, served with a vinegar-based, red cabbage slaw. With every generation there have been alterations, both necessary and accidental. When Julia moved to Vienna, she had to adapt the recipe to the locally available ingredients. So, while this version might be the first one published, it certainly is currently only the latest in a long list of adjustments and personalizations, past and future.

1 The celery seeds help get closer to the recipe's original flavor but if you can't find them, leave them out.
2 You can use any pieces of chicken you want, just plan to have about 12 pieces in total.
3 Bonne Maman jam is a family favorite for this recipe but any brand will do. Just be sure it is not finely puréed and has some texture.
4 The foil should be tightly wrapped around the edges of your baking dish but should not touch the top of the chicken or sauce.
5 The chicken tastes exponentially better the next day, the time really allows the flavors to develop. Of course, if you're short on time and need to do this all in one go, after finishing step 6, continue directly to step 9.

Let's Just Be

Friends Chicken

Let's Just Be Friends Chicken

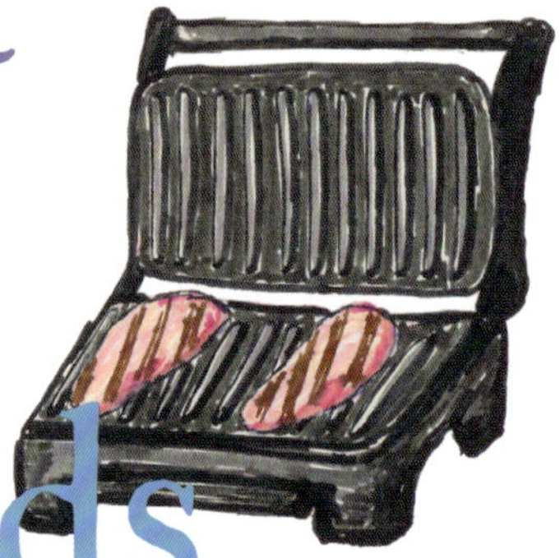

Caesar Salad

Whatever term you might have previously used to define the relationship between you and the person (or people) you're cooking for, this salad will help you to reach the platonic plateau. This is not a break-up dish but rather an appreciative invite to the next stage of the relationship. It is a Caesar salad that protects the bonds you have already made. Simple, but with strong and familiar flavors, do be sure your dining guest(s) appreciate garlic, otherwise your message might be taken the wrong way. Great on casual weekday nights this salad is not really a showstopper for extravagant dinner parties but people WILL lose their shit over it... of course, platonically.

Makes 4 servings

For the Croutons

1 loaf crusty white bread like ciabatta or baguette
2–3 tbs (30–45 ml) olive oil
kosher salt and freshly ground black pepper
1–2 garlic cloves, whole peeled

For the Dressing & Salad

2 heads of romaine lettuce
8 garlic cloves, whole peeled[1]
1 tsp (3 g) kosher salt
freshly ground black pepper
2 tbs + 2 tsp (40 ml) Worcestershire sauce
5 tbs (75 ml) red wine vinegar
1 ½–2 cups (360–480 ml) olive oil
1 piece (whole) aged Parmigiano Reggiano

For the Chicken

2 boneless, skinless chicken breasts
2 tbs (30 ml) olive oil
kosher salt & freshly ground black pepper
1 sprig of fresh rosemary, leaves removed and chopped

1. Start with your croutons.
Preheat the oven to 320°F (160°C).

2. Cut the bread into bite-sized pieces and place on a baking tray. We also like to partially cut and partially tear the bread with our hands so that you get more craggy, uneven edges.

3. Drizzle the bread with the olive oil and then sprinkle it with salt and pepper. Toss to coat.

4. Toast your croutons in the oven for about 10–15 minutes, flipping halfway so they brown evenly. Let them go as long as they need until they're nicely golden.

5. Once crispy (we still like when they have a bit of chew in the center) remove from the oven. While still warm, take a whole peeled garlic clove and gently rub all sides of the croutons. Repeat until all the bread is generously garlicky, you'll use one or two cloves here.

6. Wash and dry the lettuce. Tear into large pieces by hand and set aside.

7. In a food processor add the garlic cloves and the salt and grind to a paste.[2] Continue by adding the Worcestershire sauce, red wine vinegar and black pepper, pulse to combine and to continue breaking down the garlic.

8. Afterwards, with the motor running, slowly start drizzling in the olive oil.[3] The amount you add depends on personal taste. Stop after about a cup to check the flavor and consistency. If it's still too 'sharp' turn the motor back on and keep drizzling in more.[4] Set aside.

1 We know what you're thinking – 8 garlic cloves seems nuts, but trust us.

2 If you don't have a food processor, don't worry, a stick-immersion blender or regular blender will do the job. If you are using one of these just be sure to break down the garlic and salt first – either with a knife on your cutting board or with a mortar and pestle, before adding everything to the blender.

3 It's important to add the oil slowly and have the motor run continuously, in order to achieve a nicely thickened, emulsified, silky dressing.

4 Keep in mind, the sharpness is nicely balanced by the fresh lettuce and the rich cheese.

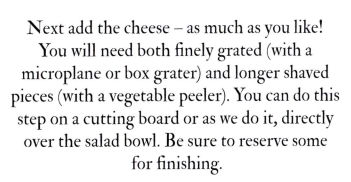

9. Cook your chicken breasts in any way that feels casual and platonic to you. For example: on the stove, heat a pan with olive oil. Season your chicken with salt, pepper and some chopped rosemary, and cook a few minutes on each side until done. Or, on the grill, do essentially the same but be sure to drizzle that oil over the chicken itself when seasoning. Whatever your method, let the chicken rest for about 10 minutes before slicing.

10. Assemble your salad. Since it has probably been sitting for a few minutes now, give your dressing a quick stir before adding a few spoonfuls of it to the bottom and sides of a large serving bowl. Top with your lettuce and croutons. Pour over some more of your dressing and give a quick toss.

11. Next add the cheese – as much as you like! You will need both finely grated (with a microplane or box grater) and longer shaved pieces (with a vegetable peeler). You can do this step on a cutting board or as we do it, directly over the salad bowl. Be sure to reserve some for finishing.

12. Toss everything together and taste, add more dressing if needed.

13. Finally, top the salad with your chicken, a final spoonful of dressing, your reserved cheese (again both finely grated and shaved) and some freshly ground black pepper.

I Want to Move in Chicken

I Want to Move in Chicken

CHICKEN POT PIE

Sometimes one wonders: how hard can it be to have a key copied? Breaking down the logistics of a move may not be the only hurdle to overcome. Let this dish do the heavy lifting. Our pot pie lays a foundation of coziness and is there to help you set the tone of your proposal. Persuasive in its warmth and generosity, consider it a glimpse into your future: one where your toothbrushes share a bathroom, rent is divided, and your houseplants mingle on the windowsill.

MAKES 4–5 SERVINGS
FOR THE PIE

- 1 half chicken cut in pieces (1 breast, 1 leg and 1 thigh) skin-on, bone-in
- 2 shallots, thinly sliced
- 4 GARLIC CLOVES, FINELY CHOPPED
- 1 medium fennel bulb, cut in half & sliced
- 3 stalks celery, sliced
- 1 tbs (2.5 g) fresh thyme leaves, chopped
- 1 tbs (3 g) fresh sage leaves, chopped
- 1 pear, medium diced
- ½ cup (120 ml) white wine
- ¼ cup (30 g) AP flour
- 1–2 cups (240–480 ml) chicken broth[1]
- kosher salt and freshly ground black pepper, to season
- 1 package puff pastry
- 1 egg, beaten for egg wash

1.
Prep all of your ingredients.

2.
Season chicken with salt and pepper. Heat cast iron pan and add olive oil.[2] When hot, add your chicken pieces and turn the heat down to medium or medium-low. The goal here is to render the fat and brown the skin while also cooking the meat. Don't rush this! After about 8 minutes, flip and sear the other side for about 10 minutes.

3.
Once cooked through, remove the chicken from the pan and let rest.

4.
Preheat the oven to 425°F (220°C).

5.
With the pan still on the stove over medium heat, add your shallots, garlic and season with a pinch of salt and black pepper. If the pan seems a bit too dry you can add a drizzle of olive oil. Cook for about 4–5 minutes, stirring until softened and beginning to get a bit of color.

6.
Add your fennel, celery and thyme. Season again with more salt and pepper and cook for another 5–8 minutes.

7.
Add wine and cook for about a minute, stirring until evaporated by half.

8.
Add the flour and stir constantly for 3–4 minutes until lightly toasted. This step will make the mixture quite thick and goopy. Do not worry!

9.
Now is the time to thin out the flour mixture by pouring in chicken broth a little at a time, stirring constantly to incorporate.[3] Turn off the heat.

10.
The chicken should now be cool enough to handle. Remove the meat from the bones and shred with your hands. Don't forget to include the crispy skin you worked hard to achieve! Discard the bones.

11.
Now add your shredded chicken, the pear and sage to the pan. Mix to combine and season to taste. Let it cool for a few minutes.

12.
While the mixture cools, lightly flour your work surface before roughly rolling your puff pastry into a circle big enough to fit over your pan.

13.
Lift the whole sheet of the dough over the top of your pan with the chicken mixture, making sure it's fully covered. Cut any larger overhanging pieces of the dough with a paring knife. Rather than cutting the edges to perfectly align with the sides of your pan, fold any excess dough over itself on top of the pie.

14.
Using your paring knife again cut three parallel slits all the way through your dough, so steam can escape during baking.

15.
With a pastry brush, brush the dough all over with the egg wash and season with a little salt and fresh pepper.

16.
Place your pan on top of a lined baking sheet and put in the middle of your oven for 30–40 minutes or until bubbling and golden brown.[4]

1 For a 10 ¼ in (26 cm) pan we used about 1 ¼ cups (300 ml) of broth.
2 A cast iron pan is a cozy way to present the pie and is preferred for the dish, but if you don't have one, another deep, oven-safe stainless steel skillet will work well too.
3 For starters it's better to keep the mixture a bit on the thicker side (yogurt consistency) as it will loosen further while baking in the oven.
4 The thing to really be sure of here is that the dough is fully cooked through. If it starts getting too brown, you can always cover it lightly with a bit of aluminum foil to finish.

LET'S TAKE SLOW CH

THINGS
CKEN

LET'S TAKE THINGS SLOW CHICKEN

SOUS VIDE CHICKEN BREAST WITH FRIED SKIN & MOLE

MAKES 4–6 SERVINGS

FOR THE CHICKEN
4–6 bone-in, skin-on chicken breasts
kosher salt and freshly ground black pepper

FOR THE MOLE
1 large tomato
½ medium yellow onion, peeled
2 limes, halved
½ large orange
2 garlic cloves, unpeeled
about 8 whole (45 g) dried pasilla chilis, stems and seeds removed
about 11 (25 g) animal crackers[1]
⅓ cup (45 g) raw or roasted peanuts
1 tbs (9 g) sesame seeds
4–5 dried allspice berries
1 star anise pod
½ tsp (1.5 g) cumin seeds
4 cups (950 ml) chicken stock
1 tbs (10 g) kosher salt[2]
2 tbs (26 g) dark brown sugar
1 chipotle chili in adobo
1.2 oz (35 g) bittersweet chocolate (75% or darker)
5 tbs (70 g) chicken schmaltz[3]

FOR THE SKIN
4–5 dashes fish sauce
1–2 tbs (7–14 g) cornstarch
freshly ground black pepper
1–2 tbs (8–15 g) AP flour
vegetable oil
honey (for garnish)
sesame seeds

IT'S HARD TO SHOW HOW MUCH YOU APPRECIATE SOMEONE WHEN YOU'RE OVERWHELMED WITH THE FEELING THAT THINGS ARE MOVING TOO QUICKLY. AS YOU PROBABLY ALREADY GUESSED, THIS DISH TAKES A WHILE TO PREPARE. DON'T WORRY SOME OF THE STEPS CAN HAPPEN IN THE BACKGROUND ALLOWING YOU TO FOCUS ON OTHER THINGS OUTSIDE OF THE KITCHEN. THE PROCESS BELOW WILL EVENTUALLY LEAD YOU TO A DELICATE YET FLAVORFUL DISH MADE UP OF SUCH DISTINCT, COMPLEMENTARY TEXTURES THAT SHOWCASE THE ADVANTAGES OF HAVING TAKEN YOUR TIME.

1.
In the morning, start by **PREPARING YOUR CHICKEN BREASTS** to be sous vide later in the day. Season them liberally with salt and pepper on both sides. Vacuum pack them in sous vide bags and put them in the refrigerator.[4]

2.
Later that day, about **3–4 HOURS BEFORE SERVING**, set a water bath with a sous vide stick to 143°F (62°C). Once the water is up to temperature, submerge the bags so that they don't interrupt the circulation of the water flow, don't touch one another and are completely covered by the water. Lightly cover the pot with a lid or foil to be sure the water doesn't evaporate over the course of cooking. Leave them to cook for anywhere between 1 ½ to 4 hours; we typically sous vide them for 2 ½ hours, which means the chicken is perfectly juicy but still has great texture.

3.
START PREPARING YOUR MOLE by measuring out the following ingredients in 3 separate bowls: in the first, add the tomato, garlic, onion, limes and orange. In the second, add your peanuts, sesame seeds, allspice, star anise and cumin. In the third, measure the brown sugar, salt and chipotle chili.

4.
Heat a cast iron or heavy bottomed pan on high. Line the bottom of the pan with two layers of aluminum foil. Char the onion, orange (flesh side down), limes (flesh side down), tomato and garlic cloves (in their skin) by leaving them on the hot aluminum-lined pan until dark. Be sure to flip the garlic, onion and tomato so they char on all sides.[5]

5.
Once this is done, add them back to their bowl, peeling the garlic cloves before doing so. Reserve two of the lime halves for garnish later.

6.
Heat 3 tbs (45 ml) of schmaltz in a large saucepan or small pot over high heat. We usually use one which is 4.6 qts (4.4 l). Once the fat is *very* hot, add the dried pasilla chilis, tossing them with tongs in the fat until they are fully coated. Let them fry in the schmaltz for 30 seconds to a minute, just until they start becoming pale in color. Use tongs to remove them from the schmaltz into a bowl. Keep most of the fat in the pot.

7.
With the pot still on the stove, add the animal crackers. Toss them constantly (for about 30–60 seconds) with your tongs until they get a dark rich golden brown color. Be careful not to burn them. Add the animal crackers to the bowl with the chilis. Again, keeping the fat in the pot.

8.
Next add your sesame seeds, star anise, cumin seeds, allspice berries and peanuts to the pot with the hot schmaltz. Let them toast in the oil for about a minute, occasionally stirring with your tongs until the sesame seeds are popping.

9.
Add the fried chilis and animal crackers back into the pot with the spices and seeds. Squeeze the juices from the charred orange half and the two lime halves into the pot before adding them into the mixture. Follow this with the blackened tomatoes, onions and peeled garlic cloves. Next add your chicken stock, sugar, salt and chipotle chili into the pot. Stir to combine, bring to a boil and then cover and reduce to a simmer for 30 minutes.

10.
After 30 minutes, set the mixture aside for about 10 minutes to allow it to cool. Remove the orange and lime pieces with tongs, squeeze out any residual liquid into the sauce and then discard them.

11.

BEGIN TO BLEND THE MIXTURE ONCE IT HAS COOLED OFF A BIT. Depending on the size of your blender and the fact that the liquid will still be warm, you probably will need to do this in batches, as hot liquids expand. Do this very carefully. Start at a low speed and then increase until you eventually blend everything on high. You want a nice, smooth consistency.

12.

Rinse out your mole pot and dry well; you will be using it again.

13.

Add 2 tbs (60 ml) chicken schmaltz to that pot and put over high heat. Once the fat is very hot, *carefully* add the puréed mole mixture to the hot fat. Stand back as it will splatter! Turn down the heat to medium and using a spatula, mix the mole into the fat, making sure to scrape the bottom and sides of the pot. Do this for 10 minutes at a medium temperature, stirring constantly. The mole will begin to turn dark, glossy and luxuriously thick.

14.

Turn off the heat. Add in your chocolate and stir until melted. Taste and add any additional salt or sugar you think it might need.

15.

Once the **CHICKEN BREASTS ARE COOKED**, remove the sous vide bags from the water bath and the chicken from the bags. Place the breasts on a cutting board. Carefully remove the skin (keep!) and discard the bones.

16.

Add the **CHICKEN SKIN** to a small bowl and pour over a few dashes of fish sauce (4–5), 1–2 tbs (7–14 g) of cornstarch and a pinch of ground black pepper. Mix together. Add 1–2 tbs (7–14 g) of flour and mix again.

17.

Add 1–2 in (2.5–5 cm) of vegetable oil to a shallow pot or pan and put over high heat.

18.

Once the oil is hot, shallow fry the chicken skin for 2–4 minutes until crispy and golden brown on both sides.

19.

Remove with tongs onto a paper towel to drain any excess fat. Season lightly with salt, add a drizzle of honey and sprinkle over some sesame seeds.

20.

TIME TO PLATE. Slice the chicken breast into about 1 in (2.5 cm) thick slices. Spoon mole onto a plate, lay your chicken on top of the sauce, finally finish the dish with the skin on top of the chicken. Serve with your reserved, charred lime wedges.[6]

1 German speakers: these are the same as *Butterkekse*, but in small animal shapes.
2 The amount of salt for your mole will largely depend on the level of salt in your stock. Start with our suggested amount and be sure to taste along the way in case you need more.
3 If you can't find chicken schmaltz see page 14 for instructions on how to make this yourself. You can also substitute with lard or neutral vegetable oil.
4 If you have time, we highly recommend seasoning the chicken breasts the night before.
5 Charring the ingredients will get your kitchen very smoky, but you need to really blacken everything in order to develop rich flavors.
6 Depending on how many chicken breasts you cook, you can cut the lime into smaller wedges or char extra halves.

Benedictus XVI
Joseph Ratzinger

I Left the Church Chicken

I Left the Church Chicken

Pope's Nose Amuse-bouche

For the Pope's Noses

12 pope's noses, cut in half and deboned[1]
2 tsp (7 g) kosher salt
1 tbs (13 g) brown sugar
1 tsp (4 g) garlic powder
2 tsp (6 g) Kashmiri chili powder
1 tsp (2.5 g) cayenne pepper
½ tsp (1.5 g) onion powder

For the Hot Sauce Jelly

¼ cup (60 ml) vinegar based, very spicy hot sauce[2]
¼ cup (60 ml) water
1 ½ tbs (14 g) gelatin powder

For the Spicy Pickled Celery

2 celery stalks, thinly sliced
½ cup (120 ml) white wine vinegar
⅛ cup (25 g) granulated sugar
½ tbs (5 g) kosher salt
2 garlic cloves, crushed
½ tbs (7 g) mustard seeds
1 tsp (2 g) red chili flakes
½ tbs (4 g) whole black peppercorns

You, our esteemed reader, may already have the impression that chicken is our religion. You're not that far off. Should you ever find yourself in the position of having to leave a religious community, here is just the right recipe to support you with the potential difficulties ahead.

The English language, just like many others, has jokingly connected one particular part of the chicken, the fleshy tail or pygostyle, to prominent pious figures. It is known as the pope's nose or the parson's nose. Both terms were invented to connect the figuratively pointed-up attitudes of the clergy with the literal upward-turned direction of a bird's tail.

We ourselves think this part of the chicken is delicious but have noticed that it often provokes a certain squeamishness and controversy leaving most diners unsure whether or not to discard the blasphemously named bite. Don't worry, there is nothing sacrilegious about going the route of replacing the pope's nose with easier-to-source, bite-sized chicken thighs.

I

Start by preparing your dry rub marinade. Mix all spices in a medium bowl and add your halved pope's nose pieces. Mix to coat evenly. Cover and let sit in the refrigerator for at least 30 minutes, although it is best left overnight.

II

Make your hot sauce jelly. Measure all ingredients into a small saucepan and stir until dissolved. Place over a stove on medium heat until liquid is very hot but not boiling, stir occasionally.

III

Remove from the heat and once cooled slightly, pour the mixture into a shallow container or Tupperware. Put in the fridge until completely set.

IV

Next up is the **pickled celery.** Place your thinly sliced pieces into a sterilized glass jar along with the garlic, mustard seeds, chili flakes and peppercorns.

V

In a small saucepan on the stove, bring the vinegar, sugar and salt to a boil. Stir until dissolved and remove from the heat. Pour the mixture into your jar with the celery and spices, being sure all pieces are submerged. Allow to cool enough to handle comfortably. Seal the lid and shake to be sure everything is well distributed. Place in the fridge to finish pickling; this takes a few hours but can be left overnight.

1 If this seems like too much trouble, 4 chicken thighs cut into small bite-sized-pieces will do the trick.
2 We like Pain is Good No. 218 Louisiana Hot Sauce.
3 This yogurt should be on the thicker side like Greek or Skyr.
4 If you're wondering what's up with all those Polish ingredients: we developed this recipe while on a residency at Villa Decius in Krakow in search of the flavors of Julia's family's past.
5 Gruszki w occie. These might be hard to find. Consider pickling your own.
6 Suska sechlońska. If you can't find these, regular dried plums will do – just consider using a smoky hot sauce.
7 If this feels too stressful to do at once, start by frying the blinis and transfer them to a baking sheet in a 200°F (90°C) preheated oven, covered loosely with some aluminum foil. This will keep them warm until serving.
8 If the butter in your buffalo sauce has started to solidify, just gently rewarm on the stove.

DAY 2

For the Corn Blinis
¼ cup (30 g) AP flour
¼ cup (42 g) coarse cornmeal (polenta)
½ tsp (2.5 g) baking powder
½ tsp (1.5 g) kosher salt
½ tbs (7.5 g) granulated sugar
1 egg
½ cup (120 ml) thick plain yogurt[3]
2 tbs (28 g) butter, melted

For the Buffalo Sauce
½ cup (120 ml) Frank's hot sauce
2 tbs (28 g) cold butter
½ tbs (7.5 ml) white wine vinegar
⅛ tsp (1 dash) Worcestershire sauce
⅛ tsp (a pinch) cayenne pepper
⅛ tsp (a pinch) garlic powder
pinch of kosher salt and freshly ground black pepper

For the Pope's Nose Dry Dredge
1 cup (120 g) AP flour
1 tbs (7 g) cornstarch
½ tsp (1.5 g) Kashmiri chili powder
pinch of kosher salt and freshly ground black pepper

For the Pope's Nose Wet Dredge
½ cup (120 ml) milk
6–8 dashes Frank's hot sauce
2 eggs

For the Garnishes
2 Polish pears in vinegar, cubed (3⁄16 in or 5 mm)[4, 5]
10–20 Polish smoked plums, cut in half lengthwise[6]
½ bunch fresh dill
honey

I
Start by making your corn blini batter. Measure flour, cornmeal, baking powder, salt and sugar into a bowl. Whisk to combine.

II
Into that same bowl, add the egg, yogurt and melted butter and whisk to combine. Cover and set aside in the fridge until later.

III
Remove the pope's noses from the fridge so they're not too cold when dredging. While they sit on the counter (for at least 30 minutes) prepare your buffalo sauce, garnishes and dredges.

IV
Make your buffalo sauce. Measure all ingredients, except for the butter, into a small saucepan and place over medium heat on the stove.

V
Slowly add the cold butter in small pieces, one at a time, whisking until combined. Take off the heat and set aside. The sauce can be slightly warmed before plating.

VI
For the garnishes finely dice the pickled pear into small 3/16 in (5 mm) cubes and set aside

VII
Cut the smoked plums in half, gently flatten and set aside.

VIII
Wash the dill. Pick off small fronds and rest to dry on a paper towel. Set aside.

IX
With a paring knife, carefully cut the hot sauce gelatin mixture into very small 3/32 in (3 mm) cubes. Set aside in the fridge.

X
Prepare your dry dredge by whisking all ingredients together in a shallow dish. Set aside.

XI
Prepare your wet dredge by whisking all ingredients together in another shallow dish. Set aside.

XII
Pat the chicken pieces dry with a paper towel.

XIII
For frying the chicken, place a heavy-bottomed pan or shallow pot, ideally cast iron, on the stove and fill with about 2 in (5 cm) of vegetable oil. Turn on the heat until the oil reaches about 350°F (176°C).

XIV
Coat the chicken first in the wet dredge, and then in the dry. Once fully covered, gently place in your hot oil and fry, on both sides, which should take about 5-7 minutes in total. Place on a wire rack to remove any excess oil and immediately season with salt. Repeat with remaining chicken pieces, being sure not to overcrowd the pan.

XV
Meanwhile, as the chicken is frying, prepare a pan for your **blinis.**[7] Heat butter or some neutral oil in a nonstick skillet over a medium flame. Form blinis by dropping about 1/2 tbs (7.5 ml) of batter per corn cake into the skillet. Fry on one side until lightly golden, flip and finish cooking. Repeat with remaining batter. Set aside on a wire rack.

XVI
Finally, to assemble! Start by laying your blinis on a serving platter and with a pastry brush, lightly spread one side with honey.

XVII
Give your buffalo sauce a stir and spoon a small amount, about 1/4-1/2 tsp (1.5-2 ml), on top of the honey.[8]

XVIII
Place one of your flattened smoked plum halves on top of the buffalo sauce.

XIX
Take one piece of your fried pope's noses and rest on top of the plum.

XX
Put one of your pear and one of your hot sauce cubes on the blini next to the chicken.

XXI
Garnish the top of your pope's nose with two slices of pickled celery and a few dill fronds.

I'VE HAD A CHANGE OF HEART CHICKEN

HOW TO
CHANGE
HEART

I'VE HAD A CHANGE OF HEART CHICKEN

CHICKEN-FILLED COCONUT MACAROONS

You are about to do something which is all planned out. Just as it starts to happen, you realize, "Oh my God no! This is going the wrong way!" Does it make sense to stick with your original intentions just because?

Having a change of heart midway into your plans might not be the smoothest course of action, instead it lays a little bit of a rocky path towards your goal. As uncomfortable as expressing your decision might be, the option to change directions could be an unexpectedly fruitful one, no matter how disruptive it appears to others (and maybe even yourself at times).

The recipe below had such a change of heart. It started out as a dumpling-filling and instead ended up being stuffed into a Jewish classic: the coconut macaroon. Should you change your mind yet again, please go ahead, another end is always possible. The meat filling is delicious over some steamed rice.

MAKES 30 MACAROONS

FOR THE
PICKLED CHILIS

½ tbs (7.5 g) granulated sugar
2 garlic cloves, crushed
½ cup (120 ml) white vinegar
1 tsp (3 g) kosher salt
¾ cup (100 g) fresh Thai red chilis, finely chopped

FOR THE
CHICKEN FILLING

¾ lb (350 g) ground chicken[1]
3 tbs (45 ml) neutral oil (veg, sunflower, corn, avocado, peanut)
2 tbs (30 ml) water
1 tbs (5 g) fresh ginger, minced
1 large onion, minced
1 tbs (15 ml) soy sauce
½ tbs (7.5 ml) dark soy sauce
1 tbs (15 ml) oyster sauce
1 tbs (15 ml) hoisin sauce
1 tsp (3 g) Chinese five spice
½ tsp (2 g) MSG
1 tsp (5 ml) sesame oil
1 tsp (5 g) granulated sugar
1 ½ tsp (3.5 g) cornstarch
1 scallion, finely chopped
1 tsp (5 g) pickled chilis, chopped
kosher salt, to taste

FOR THE
MACAROON BATTER

2 2/3 cups (260 g) sweetened coconut flakes
¾ cup (140 g) cooked sticky rice, prepare according to package instructions
¾ cup + 2 tbs (200 ml) unsweetened evaporated milk
2 egg whites
½ tsp (1.5 g) kosher salt

FOR THE
DIPPING SAUCE

2 tbs (30 ml) soy sauce
2 tbs (30 ml) Chinese black vinegar
1 large pinch of finely chopped cilantro

1.
Begin by making your pickled chilis. Wearing gloves (!), finely chop the chilis and place them in a sterilized glass jar with the garlic cloves.

2.
In a small saucepan, add the rest of your pickling ingredients and turn up the heat until it just simmers and the sugar and salt have dissolved.

3.
Turn off the heat and pour your vinegar mixture into the jar over the chilis and garlic. Let it cool a bit on the counter, close the jar and store in the fridge. The chilis will be ready to use 3 hours later or the next day.

4.
Once the chilis are pickled, start on the chicken filling. Add the chicken to a bowl and mix in 2 tbs (30 ml) cold water, a little at a time, stirring vigorously until fully incorporated.

5.
Heat 2 tbs (30 ml) of oil in a wok or stainless steel skillet. Cook the ground chicken until it turns pale and opaque, stirring and seasoning with a pinch of salt – no need to brown the meat. Once cooked through, put aside in a bowl.

6.
Add the remaining 1 tbs (15 ml) oil to your pan and sauté the minced onions for around 3–4 minutes until they start to brown. Add in the ginger and cook for 1–2 minutes until fragrant.

7.
Return the cooked chicken into the pan with the soy sauce, dark soy sauce, oyster sauce, hoisin sauce, Chinese five spice, MSG, sesame oil and granulated sugar. With the heat on medium-high, cook for 1–2 minutes until everything is combined and all the little bits of chicken are coated in the sauce.

8.
In a small bowl make a cornstarch slurry by stirring 1 tbs (15 ml) water into the cornstarch and mixing together. Pour it into the chicken mixture, stir and allow it to come to a simmer, which will take between 30 seconds and 1 minute. Remove from heat.

1 You can buy chicken already ground but it really is better, in this case, to chop it very finely by hand. If you do this, thighs, breasts or a combination of the two are fine.

2 We like to use a tablespoon for the macaroon batter and a melon baller for the chicken mixture to achieve equal amounts each time.

9.
Once your mixture has cooled, stir in the chopped scallions and the chopped pickled chilis.

10.
Preheat the oven to 355 °F (180 °C).

11.
For the macaroon batter, in a large mixing bowl measure the coconut flakes and sticky rice. With your hands, coat the rice with the coconut. This will take some time – you will need to work the coconut through the rice, breaking it up into small crumbs the size of *almost individual grains*.

12.
Once the two are well combined, add in your ¼ tsp (a big pinch) of salt and the unsweetened evaporated milk. Mix to combine.

13.
Whisk the egg whites in a stand mixer, along with ¼ tsp (a big pinch) of salt until they form soft peaks.

14.
With a rubber spatula, fold the egg whites into the coconut mixture.

15.
Time to form the macaroons. Scoop out a small amount of the coconut batter, about a tablespoon, and flatten it in the palm of your hand.[2] Then, take an even smaller amount, about a teaspoon, of the chicken mixture and place it in the center of the batter.

16.
Close your hand to make a light fist around the chicken mixture. Release and press the dough to fully cover the chicken. You can add a bit more of the coconut mixture to any holes that form. Place your macaroon on a baking paper lined cookie tray. Repeat and put in the oven for 10–12 minutes, or until the macaroons are slightly golden brown on the top.

17.
Make your dipping sauce. Finely chop cilantro. In a small bowl, mix the soy sauce and black vinegar. Sprinkle the cilantro on top.

18.
Serve macaroons with sauce on the side.

YOU WERE OUR BACKUP PLAN CHICKEN

YOU WERE OUR BACKUP PLAN CHICKEN

Basic Roast Chicken

From the infinite possibilities of roasting a delicious chicken, the method we've used here is so straightforward we could cook it in our sleep. Prepare it enough times and it will be your easy go-to meal whenever your (non-vegan, non-vegetarian) friends decide to invite themselves over at the last minute. The real comforting magic of this dish comes in when other dishes have failed you and you need something that's quick, easy and feels special every time. This is the chicken that has your back.

The potatoes underneath are 100% optional but incredibly delicious since they roast in the flavors of the chicken fat, garlic and lemon. You can also substitute them for whatever other vegetables you have in the fridge, or none at all but why not get an easy, schmaltzy, bonus side dish out of your efforts? The bird can be filled with some herbs if you have any on hand but they're not necessary. For a bit of freshness, this goes extremely well with arugula or, let's be real, any lettuce dressed with lots of herbs, lemon and olive oil. Again, use whatever you have in the fridge; the bird is your star.

MAKES 4 SERVINGS
For Your One-Pan Roast

1 3 lb (1.5 kg) chicken[1]
1 lemon, cut in quarters
2–3 handfuls of small waxy potatoes
1 head of garlic, cut in half
olive oil
kosher salt
freshly ground black pepper

Σ

PLAN A | BACKUP | PLAN C | PLAN D

YOU WERE OUR BACKUP PLAN CHICKEN

PLAN A | BACKUP | PLAN C | PLAN D

YOU WERE OUR BACKUP PLAN CHICKEN

1. **Preheat your oven** to 425°F (220°C).
2. **Start by preparing your potatoes.** Depending on their size, cut them in half or quarters. Toss them on a sheet tray or cast iron pan with two of the lemon quarters and half of the head of garlic. You can break apart the cloves a bit but don't worry about removing the skin. Drizzle with olive oil and season with a sprinkling of salt and a few cracks of ground black pepper.
3. **Pat all sides of the chicken dry** with paper towels. Don't skip this step – it's what helps with browning the skin. Season inside the cavity with plenty of salt and pepper. Then fill with the two remaining lemon quarters and the other half of the head of garlic. Rest the chicken on top of the potatoes.
4. Rub the outside of the chicken with olive oil and sprinkle generously with salt and pepper (the under-side too). Adjust the position of the chicken on the potatoes so it sits as flat as possible. Tie the legs together with a piece of butcher's twine so they're snug against the bird.[2]

PLAN A | BACKUP | PLAN C | PLAN D

5. **Place in the middle of the oven** and roast until a meat thermometer reads 160–165°F (71–74°C) in the thickest part of the thigh. For an accurate reading, be sure not to hit a bone. Our oven is insanely fast and usually takes only 35 minutes. Austrian organic chickens are on the smaller side, so depending on the size of your bird and the condition of your oven, it might take closer to an hour. That's fine, just check every 10 minutes or so and put it back in the oven until it reaches the correct temperature.[3]
6. After you remove it from the oven, carefully lift the chicken from the sheet tray or cast iron pan with a pair of tongs and let the juices from the cavity pour over the potatoes. Move the chicken to a cutting board to rest and put the potatoes back in the oven to brown a bit more (10–15 minutes). Toss the potatoes about halfway through. You can also do this step under the broiler.
7. Once the potatoes are done and the chicken is well-rested, **carve the bird** and serve with a few potatoes, some of the juices from the pan and a squeeze of lemon.

(1) The recipe will work with smaller and bigger birds, you just need to adjust timings for the size of your chicken. A thermometer is a really handy tool for this, as you can rely on the temperature of the thigh 160–165°F (71–74°C) to know when to take it out to rest.
(2) This is not a recipe for achieving super crispy skin. The point is to render the fat, which flavors the meat. The skin should still get golden brown and will taste delicious.
(3) The dark meat should eventually come up to 165°F (74°C) but this will happen while it's resting on your cutting board.

I'm Very Sick Chicken

I'm Very Sick Chicken

Matzo Ball Soup

This recipe for matzo ball soup – or 'Jewish Penicillin' as it is commonly known – is based on Julia's Nana Trudy's, with a little proportion advice from Alison Roman. Trudy's broth calls for a whole chicken, but that meat is not served in the final dish. The breast is removed earlier in the process (so it doesn't get too dry) and can be shredded and used to make delicious chicken salad (page 120 Goodbye Chicken).

Makes 6–8 servings

• For the Broth

1 3lb (1.5 kg) whole chicken, cut in pieces
several bone-heavy chicken parts (for example 5 wings or 1–2 chicken backs)
3 ½ quarts / 14 cups (3.3 l) water
1 large onion (or 2 small), cut in half
4 carrots, roughly diced
3 celery stalks, roughly diced
1 bunch (30 g) dill (and stems)
2 bunches (60 g) parsley (and stems)
2–3 *big* pinches kosher salt
1 ½ tsp (4 g) whole black peppercorns

• For the Matzo Balls

1 cup (116 g) matzo meal
1 ¾ tsp (5.5 g) kosher salt
5 eggs
⅓ cup (75 g) chicken schmaltz
¼ cup (60 ml) seltzer

• For the Garnish

2–3 carrots, diced into bite-sized cubes
1 handful dill, chopped
1 handful parsley, chopped

- **Start by making your chicken broth.**[1] Place the chicken in a large pot and cover with the cold water. Bring to a boil. After about 10 minutes, use a spoon to skim off any foam floating on top.
- Add in the rest of your ingredients, bring back up to a boil and cover, turning it down to a heavy simmer.
- About 30 minutes in, remove the chicken breasts. Turn down to a light simmer and cook for another hour and a half.
- Remove the rest of the chicken from the pot and transfer to a plate.
- Strain broth into another pot.
- Mash the carrot, celery and onion (a few at a time) through a fine mesh metal strainer with a wooden or metal spoon. Scrape the solids from the bottom of the strainer directly into the pot with the broth, discarding the herbs and peppercorns as you go. Taste and season with more salt, if necessary.
- Let the broth cool to room temperature before putting it in the fridge overnight.
- **Next make the matzo ball batter.** Mix the matzo meal and salt in a medium bowl. Add the eggs and whisk.
- Add the chicken schmaltz and whisk to combine.
- Then, add the seltzer, whisking until fully incorporated.
- Cover with plastic wrap and place in the fridge until the batter holds together more, and the matzo meal has fully hydrated (2–24 hours).
- When you take the broth out of the fridge the next day, skim off the fat that has collected at the top while it is still cold.[2]
- Heat broth on the stove. Taste and season (with salt) accordingly.
- Bring a large pot of water to boil, salt well.
- Dice a few carrots and place them in the pot of boiling water. When slightly softened, remove carrots with a slotted spoon and set aside. Keep this water on the stove.
- Roll out the matzo mixture into ping-pong sized balls. Once round, place them on a plate or baking sheet. Depending on how large you make them, you should get 18-20 balls.[3]
- Quickly roll the matzo balls back into shape before gently placing them in the pot of boiling water. Cook until they float to the top and have almost doubled in size (12–15 minutes).
- Using a slotted spoon, transfer the matzo balls directly into the chicken broth.
- Finely chop some parsley and dill.
- **For serving** add 1 or 2 matzo balls and broth to a bowl. Top with a few pieces of carrot, and finish with a sprinkling of the freshly chopped dill and parsley.

1 Ideally you should plan to make the broth and the matzo ball batter the day before. This allows for an easy removal of the layer of (now cooled) fat from the top of the pot of broth. Also, with extra time, the matzo meal can fully hydrate, giving the dumplings their desired fluffy texture.

2 The fat can be discarded or you can save it for future cooking!

3 While rolling out the matzo balls, it is helpful to have a bowl of water ready to wet your hands. This helps prevent the dough from sticking too much.

I Love You Chicken

I Love You Chicken

Brined Roast Chicken with Tomatoes

When you bring this dish to the table, it may appear simple; however, the attentiveness you show in its execution will make your feelings taste abundantly clear.[1]

1. Start by preparing your brining liquid. Combine all of the ingredients in a large stock pot.[3] Give them a stir and bring to a boil over high heat. Once boiling, turn off the heat and let cool. Cover and chill brine in the refrigerator.

2. When the brine is cold, fully submerge the chicken in the liquid and chill in the refrigerator, covered, for 8–12 hours.[4]

3. Once done brining, prepare a metal rack on top of a baking sheet. Remove the chicken from the pot, place it on the rack and dry it well with paper towels. Discard the brine.

4. Truss the chicken with kitchen twine.[5] You can either just tie the legs closely together, or follow the more elaborate method described in step 5.

5. Cut a 3 ft (90 cm) long piece of kitchen twine. Anchor the center of the twine under the pope's nose and wrap each end over the ends of the legs and back across, making a figure of eight. With a piece of twine in each hand, bring both ends up, along the breasts, towards the neck of the chicken. Cross the twine over the neck, eventually then tying a knot. Use the remaining ends to pull from the neck down towards the wings, tying them snugly against the body. Make a knot in the back to finish.

6. Move your well-tied chicken (still on the metal-rack-lined baking sheet) and leave uncovered, in the fridge for 2 days.[6]

7. After 2 days, remove the chicken and allow it to come to room temperature (about 30 minutes – 1 hour).

8. Once the chicken is at room temperature preheat your oven to 425°F (220°C).

9. Put the leeks, tomatoes, half of the fresh oregano sprigs and garlic into a roasting pan or cast iron pan. Season lightly with salt, pepper and olive oil. Push most of the tomatoes to the outer edges of the pan, keeping your leeks in the center.

10. Stuff the remaining half of your oregano sprigs inside the cavity of the chicken.

Makes 4 servings

For the Chicken[2]

1 3 lb (1.5 kg) chicken
7–8 small to medium tomatoes, cut in half (about 1 ½ lbs or 680 g)
1 leek, cut in half lengthwise and cut each half into 4 pieces
2 heads garlic, cut in half
2 tbs (30 g) butter, cut into small cubes
1 ½ tbs (7.5 g) fennel seed, crushed in mortar and pestle
1 small bunch (10 g) fresh oregano
2 tbs (30 ml) red wine vinegar
olive oil
kosher salt & freshly ground black pepper

For the Brine

1 small bunch (10 g) fresh oregano
2 tbs (10 g) fennel seed
4 lemons, cut in half
1 orange, cut in half
6 bay leaves
2–3 bunches (110 g) flat-leaf parsley
1 bunch (25 g) fresh thyme
¼ cup (60 ml) honey
1 head garlic, cut in half
2 tbs (15 g) whole black peppercorns
1 cup (160 g) kosher salt
1 gallon (3.8 l) water

1 *This is not a recipe for spontaneous declarations; it requires 3 days, from start to finish, to develop its full potential.*
2 *This recipe is best served with a fresh baguette and delicate, leafy green salad.*
3 *Be sure to use one large enough to eventually fit both the brine and the whole chicken. Ours is 7.6 qts (7.2 l).*
4 *If you want, go the extra step and remove the wishbone from the chicken before submerging in your brine. This step is optional, but it will make it easier to carve the chicken after it's cooked.*
5 *The point of trussing is to hold all of the parts of the chicken as closely together as possible to allow for even cooking.*
6 *Don't skip this step! You will notice over those 2 days how the color and texture of the skin will change, providing a chance for great browning later.*

11. Season the chicken liberally, on all sides, with olive oil, fennel seeds, salt and pepper.

12. Lay your chicken on top of the leeks. Dot the butter cubes evenly on top of your tomatoes.

13. With the oven preheated, place your chicken on the middle rack and roast for about 20 minutes.

14. Lower the oven temperature to 350°F (175°C) and roast for an additional 30 minutes, depending on your oven. You'll know your chicken is done when the temperature of the dark meat between the thigh and leg is 160–165°F (71–74°C) or until the juices run clear.

15. Place the roasted chicken onto a cutting board and let it rest for 10–20 minutes before carving.

16. While your chicken is resting, put the tomatoes and leeks back into the oven for about 10 minutes to allow them to darken.

17. Remove the pan from the oven, add the red wine vinegar to the tomatoes and leeks, giving them a gentle stir.

18. Carve the chicken and serve on top of the jammy tomatoes, leeks and garlic. Don't forget to spoon the delicious juices from the bottom of your pan on top of the meat when serving.

I FROZE MY EGGS CHICKEN

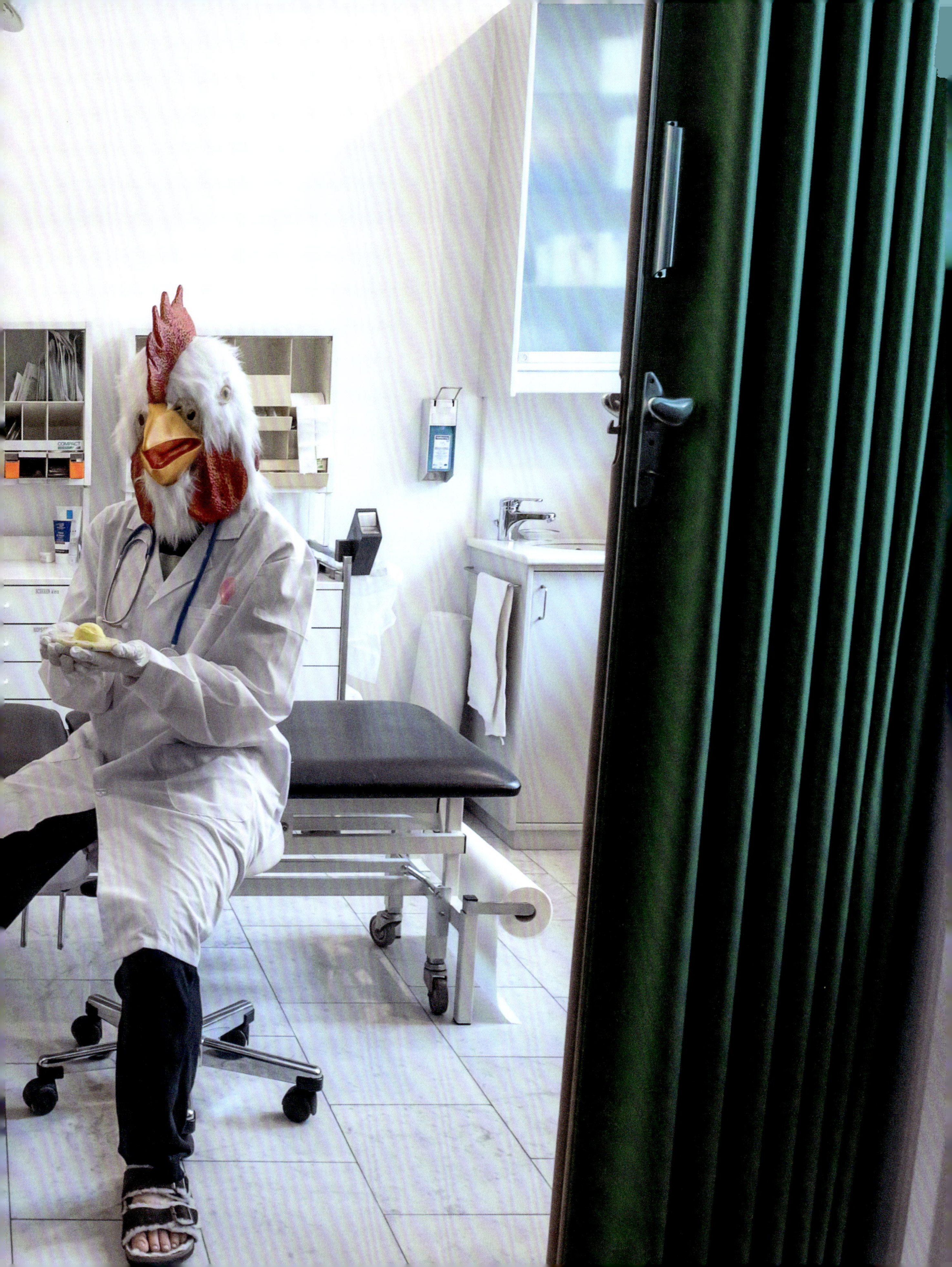

I FROZE MY EGGS CHICKEN

CHICKEN SORBET & EGG, TURMERIC, CARDAMOM ICE CREAM

UNLESS YOU FEEL LIKE SHARING, YOUR REPRODUCTIVE RIGHTS ARE NOBODY'S BUSINESS BUT YOUR VERY OWN. HOWEVER, IN CASE YOU ONE DAY SHOULD FEEL THE NECESSITY TO EXPLAIN TO SOMEONE WHY YOU DON'T IMMEDIATELY NEED TO HAVE THEIR BABY OR WHERE A BIG CHUNK OF YOUR SAVINGS HAS GONE OR WHY THIS "YOUR INNER CLOCK IS TICKING" BULLSHIT IS NOT REALLY ALWAYS A SET COOKIE-CUTTER MODEL FOR EVERYONE, WE HAVE JUST THE RIGHT DISH FOR YOU. I FROZE MY EGGS CHICKEN **IS COMPOSED OF TWO ICE CREAM FLAVORS, BEST SERVED IN A CLINICAL WAY: A GLASS PETRI DISH.**

BY THE WAY, YOU MIGHT NOTICE AS YOU INSPECT THE INGREDIENTS LIST THAT WE DON'T OFFER UP THE USUAL MEASUREMENT CONVERSIONS – IN THIS CASE IT'S BEST TO BE EXACT AND USE A SCALE.

CHICKEN SORBET & GIN INFUSION

MAKES 12–16 SERVINGS

FOR THE CHICKEN SORBET

- 0.3G GUAR GUM
- 0.3G LOCUST BEAN GUM
- 0.1G XANTHAN GUM
- 68 G DEXTROSE
- 50 G GLUCOSE
- 550 G COLD CHICKEN BROTH[1]
- 15 G GIN INFUSION
- LARGE PINCH FINELY CHOPPED PARSLEY
- SQUEEZE OF FRESH LEMON JUICE
- 2 PINCHES KOSHER SALT

FOR THE GIN INFUSION

- 300 ML GIN[2]
- 30 G PARSLEY
- ROUGHLY CHOPPED WITH STEMS
- 30 G CILANTRO SPRIGS
- ROUGHLY CHOPPED WITH STEMS
- 2 × 7.5 G N2O CHARGERS FOR ISI WHIPPER

1. Start your **chicken sorbet** by weighing and stirring the dry ingredients – the guar gum, locust bean gum, xanthan gum, dextrose and glucose – in a small bowl.
2. Add to a blender and blend with your cold chicken broth until dissolved.
3. Pour the mixture from the blender into a saucepan and heat on medium. Heating will activate the powders. Stir frequently, until the mixture just reaches 176°F (80°C). Remove from the heat and pour into a medium sized bowl. Set aside.
4. While the mixture is cooling, you have time to **make your gin infusion.** Place the gin, parsley and cilantro in an ISI whipper. Close whipper and infuse with two N2O chargers, waiting 2 ½ minutes after inserting the second one while agitating occasionally.
5. With the whipper held in the upright position, slowly release the gas from the canister, making sure not to spray out the liquid. After the pressure has been released, unscrew the lid and wait a few minutes until the bubbling sounds have disappeared. Strain through a fine mesh strainer and discard the remaining herbs.
6. Now that the chicken stock mixture has come to room temperature, add 15 ml of the gin infusion, a small squeeze of lemon, two pinches of salt and some very finely chopped parsley to the bowl. Stir to combine and dissolve the salt.
7. Cover and let rest in the fridge overnight.
8. **The next day,** pour the cold sorbet base into your ice cream machine and let spin until it reaches the consistency of a frozen, smooth sorbet. This varies by machine but it takes ours about 15 minutes.
9. Transfer your sorbet to a container and store in the freezer until ready to serve.

1 We highly recommend using homemade broth. See page 70 for our matzo ball soup recipe.

2 It works best with high-proof alcohol. We used Tanqueray, 47% vol.

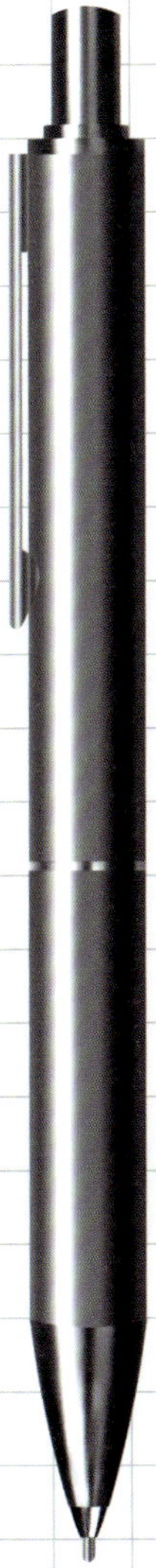

- 200 ML CREAM
- 400 ML MILK
- 120 G GRANULATED SUGAR
- 6 EGG YOLKS
- PINCH OF KOSHER SALT
- 2.5 G TURMERIC POWDER
- 3-4 CARDAMOM PODS, CRUSHED

FOR THE EGG, TURMERIC, CARDAMOM ICE CREAM

EGG, TURMERIC, CARDAMOM ICE CREAM

1. **Start by making your ice cream base.** Crush the cardamom pods with a mortar and pestle or the side of your knife and add to a small saucepan with the milk, cream, turmeric, 25 g of the sugar and a pinch of salt. Stir and place over medium heat until it just reaches 176°F (80°C). Remove from heat.
2. Put the egg yolks into a bowl and whisk with the remaining sugar until dissolved.
3. Prepare an ice bath by filling a large bowl with ice and cold water and place a medium bowl into the ice bath, being sure not to get water into the second bowl. Place a fine mesh strainer nearby.
4. Temper your yolks by slowly pouring about half of the milk mixture into the yolks, whisking constantly. This method helps prevent the yolks from scrambling.
5. Pour yolk mixture into the saucepan with the remaining spiced milk and whisk constantly over low heat until thickened and the temperature reaches 176°F (80°C). This should take about 3 minutes.
6. Quickly, remove the ice cream base from the heat and strain it into the bowl resting in the ice bath. Discard any egg solids and cardamom pods collected by the strainer. You want to cool down the mixture quickly and evenly. To do so, stir constantly with a rubber spatula, scraping the sides of the bowl in the process.
7. Once cooled, cover and leave to rest in the fridge overnight.
8. **The next day,** pour the cold ice cream base into the ice cream machine and let spin until frozen and creamy. This varies by machine, but ours takes about 15–20 minutes.
9. Transfer your ice cream to a container and store in the freezer until ready to serve.
10. **Time to plate!** In a glass petri dish, make a base by evenly spreading out some of your chicken sorbet. We like an offset spatula for this. Top it with a small scoop of your egg ice cream and serve immediately.

LET'S
BE
BENEFITS

FRIENDS WITH CHICKEN

LET'S BE BENEFITS

ds are sexy.
e are a few reasons why this one is:

FRIENDS WITH CHICKEN

a) *It satiates without holding your stomach hostage.*

b) *Crisp, wide lettuce leaves can whet the appetite; especially when torn by hand.*

c) *Arousing dental crunches from overwhelmingly different textures will tease your senses bite by bite.*

d) *The flavors from vinegar and the lusciousness from oil can playfully awaken the taste buds, teasing and tantalizing with its delightful acidity. Vinaigrette could be a cute pet name worth whispering into someone's ear.*

e) *The mysteriously forbidden depths of pumpkin seed oil will always bear the risk of staining. Don't forget to use protection.*

Backhendl Salat

MAKES 6 SERVINGS

FOR AUSTRIAN POTATO SALAD

3–3 ½ LBS (1.5 KG) SMALL WAXY POTATOES, WHOLE
SCANT 1 CUP (100 G) RED ONION, VERY FINELY CHOPPED
2 CUPS (480 ML) BEEF BROTH
¼ CUP + 2 TBS (90 ML) WHITE WINE VINEGAR
2 TSP (7 G) KOSHER SALT
¼ CUP + 2 TBS (90 ML) VEGETABLE OIL
FRESHLY GROUND BLACK PEPPER

FOR SALAD & DRESSING

2 TBS (34 G) DIJON OR TARRAGON MUSTARD
2 CLOVES OF GARLIC, GRATED
2 TBS (30 ML) PUMPKIN SEED OIL
4 TBS (60 ML) BALSAMIC VINEGAR
PINCH OF KOSHER SALT, FRESHLY GROUND BLACK PEPPER
4 TBS (12 G) CHIVES, FINELY CHOPPED
2 HEADS RED LEAF LETTUCE, TORN IN LARGE PIECES
2–3 HANDFULS LAMB'S LETTUCE
5–6 RADISHES, SLICED
5–6 CHERRY OR PLUM TOMATOES, HALVED
1 RED ONION, VERY THINLY SLICED
PUMPKIN SEEDS, FOR FINISHING
EXTRA PUMPKIN SEED OIL, FOR FINISHING
CHIVES, FINELY CHOPPED FOR FINISHING

FOR BREADED CHICKEN

1 CUP (240 ML) YOGURT (OR BUTTERMILK)
1 ½ LB (680 G) CHICKEN BREAST, CUT IN STRIPS
1 CUP (120 G) AP FLOUR
3 EGGS, BEATEN
2 CUPS (100 G) PANKO
½ CUP (60 G) CRUSHED PUMPKIN SEEDS
VEGETABLE OIL FOR SHALLOW FRYING

1. **Prepare ahead:** *Slice chicken breasts into thin strips and place in a medium sized mixing bowl. Add the yogurt and a pinch of salt and pepper. Mix well, cover and set in the fridge overnight or for at least 4–5 hours.*

2. *On the day you want to serve this dish, begin by removing your chicken from the fridge and then get started on your* **potato salad**. *Place potatoes in a large stockpot covering them with cold water and a handful of salt.*[1] *Place a lid on the pot and bring to a boil.*
3. *Once boiling, turn the heat down to a simmer and cook until fork-tender, about 20 minutes, depending on the size of your potatoes.*
4. *Drain and let cool just enough to handle, but still warm.*
5. *While the potatoes begin to cool make the 'marinade'. Heat the beef broth in a small saucepan over medium heat and add in the vinegar, onions, salt and pepper. Once simmering, turn off the heat.*
6. *Peel the potatoes with a small paring knife and cut into slices, placing them in a heatproof bowl. If your marinade has cooled down a lot, quickly heat it up again on the stove and then pour it over the potatoes. Ideally you want the potatoes to be slightly warm and the marinade to be hot.*
7. *Let this mixture sit for about 30 minutes, stirring every so often with a rubber spatula.*[2]
8. *After 30 minutes, add in the vegetable oil and any additional salt and pepper to taste. Stir again, allowing the potatoes to break up a bit and the whole mixture to become somewhat creamy. Set aside on the counter.*
9. **Next make your salad dressing.** *In a small mixing bowl, finely grate the cloves of garlic. Add in the mustard, pumpkin seed oil, balsamic vinegar, salt and pepper and whisk to combine. Set aside.*
10. *Place your washed, dried and torn* **lettuce** *in a large bowl along with the lamb's lettuce and set aside. Make sure your other sliced veggies are prepped and standing by as you will need them soon.*
11. **Prepare a breading station for the chicken.** *You will need three shallow dishes. Put your flour in one, in another the beaten eggs and in the third your panko breadcrumbs mixed with the chopped pumpkin seeds. Season each of them with a pinch of salt and some fresh black pepper, stirring to combine.*
12. *Heat a shallow layer (1–2 in or 3–5 cm) of oil in a pan or pot with low sides. Prepare a wire rack over a few layers of paper towels for when your chicken pieces come out of the oil.*
13. **Begin breading your chicken,** *one strip at a time. Coat each strip fully in the flour, then the egg and finally the panko/pumpkin seed mixture. You can use a bit of pressure to press the panko crumbs onto the egg, to be sure they're well covered.*
14. **Fry your chicken strips** *(making sure not to overcrowd the pan) until golden brown on all sides and cooked through. This should take about 4–6 minutes total.*

15. *As soon as the chicken is done frying, move with tongs to your wire rack and immediately season with a sprinkling of salt. Continue the process until all of your chicken is cooked.*
16. *Finally,* **assemble your salad.**[3] *Add some dressing to the lettuce in your mixing bowl, toss and taste, adding more if needed.*
17. *On a dinner plate, place a few spoonfuls of your potato salad, add lettuce next before scattering some radish slices and tomato halves on top. Follow this with two to three pieces of your chicken. On top, add some shaved red onion, a sprinkling of finely chopped chives and pumpkin seeds. Lastly, lightly drizzle everything with a little extra pumpkin seed oil and serve.*

1 THE POTATOES SHOULD BE KEPT WHOLE AS LONG AS THEY ARE ROUGHLY THE SAME SIZE, TO ENSURE EVEN COOKING. IF SOME ARE MUCH LARGER THAN THE REST, CUT THEM IN HALF.

2 IF YOU'RE NOT FAMILIAR WITH AUSTRIAN POTATO SALAD IT MIGHT SEEM LIKE THE POTATOES ARE DROWNING IN TOO MUCH LIQUID. DON'T WORRY, THEY WILL SOAK UP MOST OF THE MARINADE OVER TIME.

3 THIS IS NOT A SALAD TO BE TOSSED ALL AT ONCE AND SERVED FAMILY STYLE. IT IS BEST ASSEMBLED AND GARNISHED ON INDIVIDUAL PLATES.

I HATE YOU CHICKEN

Fancy Feast

I HATE YOU CHICKEN SALMONELLA SPELL

Makes up to Infinite Servings

WHEN YOU HAVE GONE THROUGH ALL STAGES OF DISLIKE AND FINALLY REACHED THE NEXUS OF HATE, THE LAST THING YOU WANT TO DO IS COOK FOR THE PERSON WHO TRIGGERS SUCH EMOTIONS. DON'T WORRY THOUGH, THIS OFFERING DOESN'T MEAN YOU HAVE TO SEE THEM AGAIN AS WE DEVELOPED A LONG-DISTANCE SOLUTION WITH LITTLE TO NO COOKING TIME. I HATE YOU CHICKEN IS INVESTED IN THE COMFORT OF ITS EXECUTOR AND THE DISCOMFORT OF THE PERSON IT'S DIRECTED TOWARDS.

salmonella

I hate you chicken
salmonella

Of a chicken take any part-
It may be minced, it may be whole
or fall apart - take a pinch of
what the hated detests - it may
be raisins, papaya, cilantro, a duck's
breasts - add a scoop of chicken cat
food and a piece of ginger root.
Stir well with the feather of a hen's back
now you're almost ready to launch your
attack. Howl with your deepest voice the
fateful word twice: Salmonella!
Salmonella! Then backwards and
precise: Allenomlas! Allenomlas!
Think of the hated with a shiver -
one last time your heart will quiver.
From now on Salmonella will befall the hated
every sight of chicken be ill-fated

MEET

PARENTS

MY
CHICKEN

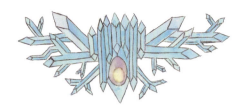

MEET MY PARENTS CHICKEN

DEVILED EGGS & CHOPPED LIVER

When introducing your partner to your parents, whose judgment are you more nervous about? While many families have a very welcoming attitude towards new additions, you, our reader, are perhaps turning to this recipe because you're already anticipating that someone will misbehave. Support your walk on eggshells with this combination of new and familiar flavors.

Deviled eggs and chopped chicken liver are classics for a reason. And while we certainly aren't the first to revamp these dishes, they can serve as a great foundation for this ceremonial act of meeting the parents. Even if everything falls apart, this dish is a great pick-me-up for you and your loved one to process the encounter.

Makes 6–8 servings

FOR THE PICKLED EGGS

1 cup (240 ml) red wine vinegar
1 cup (240 ml) water
4 or 5 allspice berries
1 tsp (2.5 g) whole black peppercorns
½ tbs (7 g) yellow mustard seeds
1 tbs (15 g) granulated sugar
1 tsp (1.5 g) dried dill
pinch of kosher salt
8 eggs
1 cooked red beet

FOR THE CHOPPED LIVER

1 lb (500 g) chicken livers
¼ cup (55 g) chicken schmaltz, see page 14
2 yellow onions, thinly sliced
1–2 hard boiled eggs[1]
kosher salt
and freshly ground black pepper
1 red onion, finely diced

FOR THE PICKLED MUSTARD SEEDS

½ cup (100 g) yellow mustard seeds
½ cup + 2 tbs (150 ml) rice wine vinegar
¼ cup + 2 tbs (90 ml) water
¼ cup + 2 tbs (90 ml) mirin
¼ cup (50 g) granulated sugar
½ tbs (5 g) kosher salt

FOR THE DEVILED EGG FILLING

8 hard boiled egg yolks
1 tsp (7 g) red miso
½ cup (110 g) mayonnaise
freshly ground black pepper
2 pinches of kosher salt
gribenes (crispy chicken skin),[2]
see page 14

1 Eggs in Austria aren't as big as they are in the US. In this recipe we usually use almost 2 full eggs. If you have extra large eggs, start with 1 and after blending in the food processor taste and see if you want to add more.
2 Gribenes, or the crispy fried chicken skin you get when rendering schmaltz, are not only a delicious snack but great on these eggs. You will need 1–2 pieces per egg half.
3 For an easy time peeling hard boiled eggs, as soon as they're done boiling, lightly crack the shell and immediately cover in cold water. Once cool enough to handle, peel!
4 The mustard seeds will last in your fridge for about a month.

I

The day before serving, pickle your eggs. Add all pickling ingredients to a pot, bring to a boil and then remove from the heat and let cool.

II

While the pickling liquid is cooling, hard boil 8 eggs. Use your favorite method. We like to cover them in cold water, boil for 10 minutes, drain and then peel.[3]

III

Slice one cooked red beet and place in a glass jar or other non-reactive container with a tight lid along with your peeled eggs and the pickling liquid with spices. Cover and place in the fridge overnight.

IV

The next day make your schmaltz and gribenes. Set aside.

V

Next prepare your pickled mustard seeds. Place all the ingredients into a small saucepan on the stove on medium heat and bring to a gentle boil. Turn down the heat and simmer, on low, for 1 hour or until the mustard seeds are plump. Make sure to stir occasionally. Taste for seasoning and set aside to cool.[4]

VI

Time to make your chopped chicken liver. Clean your livers by cutting off any tough tendons.

VII

Add 2 tbs (30 ml) chicken schmaltz to a skillet over medium-high heat and fry half of the livers for about 3 minutes per side. Pour the livers and the fat from the skillet into a bowl and set aside.

VIII

Repeat, adding 2 more tbs (30 ml) of schmaltz to the pan and frying the second half of the livers. This time, remove only the livers, keeping the fat in the pan.

IX

Add onions to the hot skillet, toss in the chicken fat and then turn the heat to medium-low. Cover and cook for about 10 minutes, stirring once or twice to be sure the onions don't burn.

X

Uncover the skillet and with the heat set to low, cook for about 30 minutes until the onions are caramelized.

XI

Add in your garlic powder and stir before taking the skillet off the heat.

XII

Add your livers, onions, 1–2 hard boiled eggs, salt and pepper to your food processor. Pulse and then purée until the mixture starts to become smooth but still has some texture. You don't want a completely even consistency. Taste for seasoning and set aside.

XIII

Now it's time to continue with your deviled eggs. Remove your pickled eggs from the refrigerator and then from the pickling brine. On a cutting board, slice the eggs carefully in half lengthwise. Set the whites to the side and add the yolks to a fine mesh strainer set over a mixing bowl.

XIV

Push the yolks through the strainer with a wooden spoon.

XV

Add your miso, mayonnaise, salt and pepper to the yolks and mix well, until very smooth.

XVI

On a serving tray, place your egg whites cut side up. With a piping bag, fill your egg white halves with your miso-flavored yolk mixture. Garnish with a small spoonful of the pickled mustard seeds and a piece or two of your gribenes.

XVII

Transfer your chopped liver to a serving bowl and sprinkle your finely chopped red onion on top. Serve with crackers or challah.

Give Me a Secon

Chance Chicken

Give Me a Second Chance Chicken

Sloppy Chicken Sandwiches

Sometimes things get complicated:
Friendships change, fights explode, distances are stretched, boundaries are set. This is a recipe for that person in your life who you want to patch things up with. It is a noncommittal offering, easiest served in a similarly neutral setting. Meeting at the park, for example, would allow everyone involved to have the chance for an easy exit. Since the dish is made for take-out, the food can still be enjoyed even if the conversation has gone sour. Remember to bring lots of napkins, things can get messy.

This dish is all about second chances, so now is a timely opportunity for you and your chicken leftovers. You can use whatever you have left from a supermarket rotisserie chicken (if you're lucky enough to live in a place where you can get a good one) or feel free to give that Backup Plan Chicken (see page 64) a second chance as well. The amounts in this recipe refer to a whole roast chicken, even though it might be difficult to imagine having an entire leftover chicken. That being said, this is just a point of reference, so adapt the recipe to however much meat you have.

Makes 5–6 servings

For the Chicken
1 whole roasted chicken, shredded[1]
1 small yellow onion, finely diced
2 tbs (30 ml) neutral oil (veg, sunflower, corn, avocado, peanut)
½ tsp (1.5 g) chili powder[2]
1 tsp (3 g) smoked paprika
1 tsp (4 g) garlic powder
1 tsp (2.5 g) ground cumin
½ tsp (1.5 g) ground ginger
¼ tsp (a big pinch) cayenne pepper
2 tbs (30 ml) apple cider vinegar
1 ½ cups (355 g) ketchup
1 ½ tbs (20 g) brown sugar
1 ½ tbs (25 g) Dijon mustard
10 dashes Worcestershire sauce
½ tsp (1.5 g) kosher salt
¼ tsp (a big pinch) freshly ground black pepper

For the Slaw
1 medium large kohlrabi, peeled and cut into thin strips[3]
½ lemon, juiced
½ cup (25 g) parsley, roughly chopped
¼ cup (55 g) mayonnaise
1 tsp (5 g) granulated sugar
½ tsp (1.5 g) kosher salt
freshly ground black pepper

Remaining Ingredients
6 brioche burger buns
optional 2–3 tbs (28–42 g) room temperature butter

1.
Carve chicken, remove skin and bones and shred the meat with your hands. This is far superior to chopping it with a knife as it allows the sauce to permeate the meat more.

2.
To **begin the sauce** measure 2 tbs (30 ml) of oil and warm in a small saucepan over medium heat, add diced onion and a small pinch of salt.

3.
Sauté onion for 3–5 minutes, or until translucent, not brown.

4.
Add spices and stir for about a minute, reducing heat if necessary.

5.
Add the vinegar and stir for less than a minute. The liquid will bubble away and should reduce by half.

6.
Once reduced, add the ketchup, brown sugar, mustard, salt and Worcestershire sauce to the pan, along with some freshly ground black pepper. At this point, the bubbling can get a bit violent, so be sure to keep the heat down low to a casual simmer.

7.
After slowly bubbling for about 5 minutes, taste and adjust the seasonings, if necessary.

8.
Take your shredded chicken and add it directly to the pot with your sauce. Stir together and keep stirring while it remains on low heat to allow the flavors to come together. Be sure not to leave this alone too long – all the sugar in the ketchup can burn easily. Before moving to the next step, turn off the heat.

9.
Make your slaw.[4] Peel kohlrabi, cut into very thin slices either with a knife or mandolin.

10.
Lay slices on top of each other on your cutting board and cut again into very thin strips lengthwise.

11.
Add your cut kohlrabi slices to a small mixing bowl.

12.
Roughly chop the parsley and add it to the kohlrabi along with the mayo, granulated sugar, lemon juice, salt and pepper.

13.
Mix everything well and taste for seasoning.

14.
Now prepare for **assembly.** Slice the brioche buns in half.

15.
Toast the buns. You can do this lightly in a toaster, or if you want to be extra decadent, spread them with a little bit of the room temperature butter and toast in a heavy bottomed (cast iron) pan until golden brown (cut side only).

16.
Assemble the sandwiches. Pile a few spoonfuls of your chicken mixture on the bottom half of the bun, followed by some of your slaw and top with the other half of the brioche. Wrap well in wax paper and take them to go!

1 Makes enough sauce for a single whole 3 lb (1.5 kg) chicken.
2 This recipe goes quickly. We recommend pre-measuring the dried spices all together in a small bowl before starting.
3 Can't find kohlrabi? Go for some nice radishes. You just want something refreshingly crisp, crunchy and slightly peppery.
4 The kohlrabi will release liquid the longer it sits, so we recommend making this just before eating.

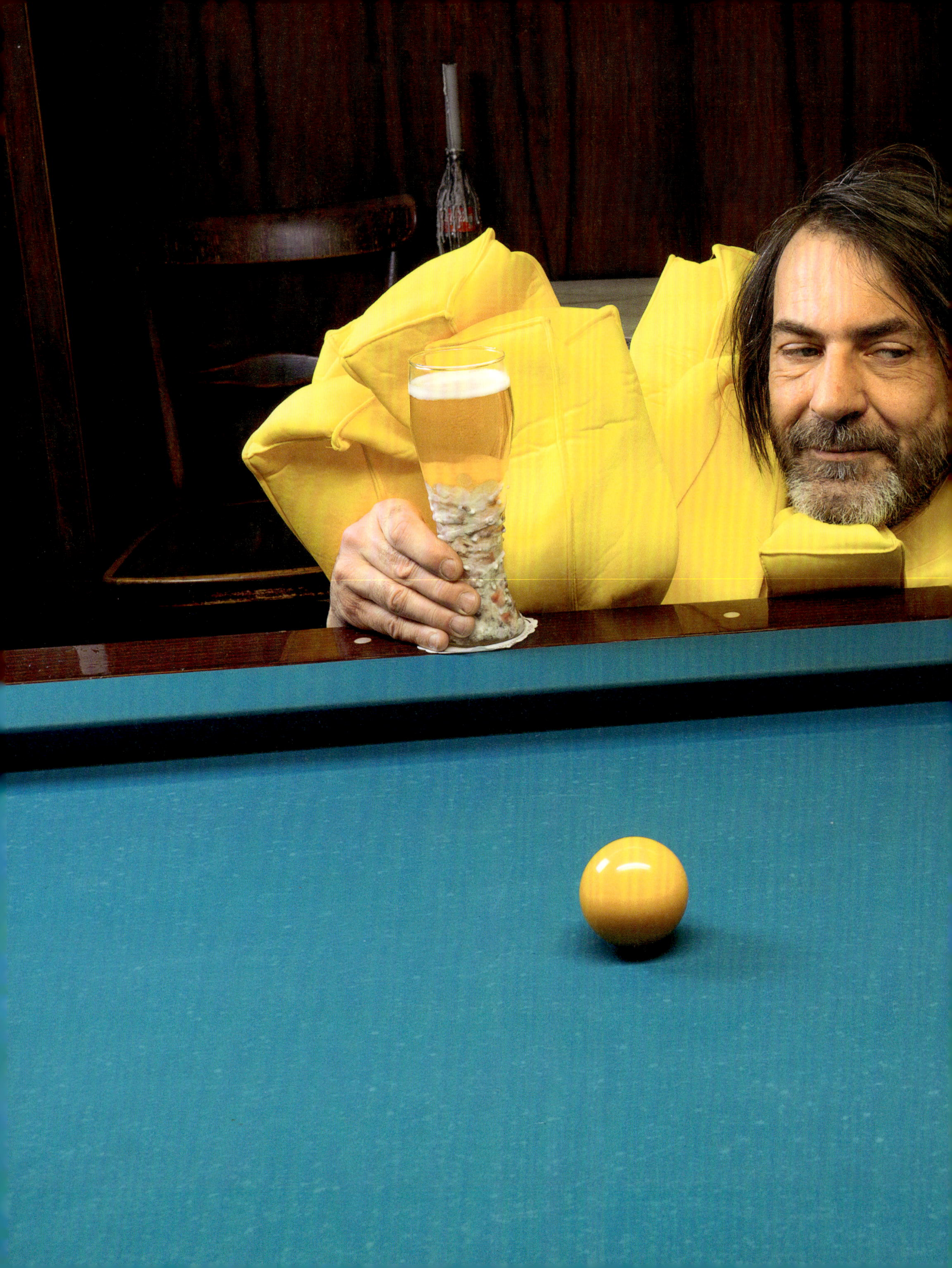

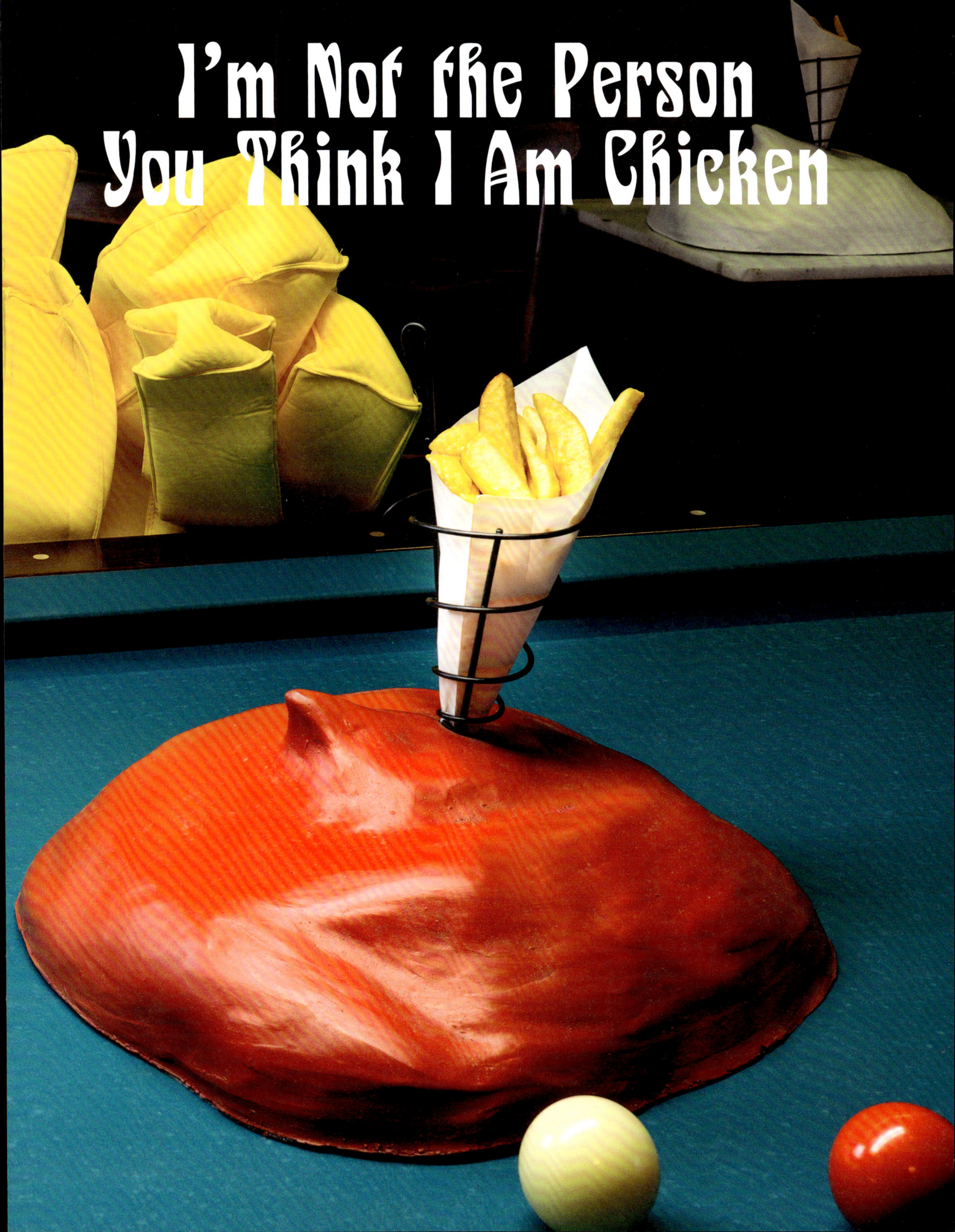
I'm Not the Person
You Think I Am Chicken

I'm Not the Person You Think I Am Chicken

Currywurst Chicken-filled French Fries with Reversed Ketchup & Mayo

Appearances can be deceiving. This twisted take on a German *Currywurst mit Pommes* combines all of the traditional ingredients of a familiar dish in duplicitous ways. The hidden surprise lies inside, offering a humorous metaphor which should make your news easier to swallow.

000
00

Makes 2–3 servings

FOR THE FRENCH FRIES

1 package of frozen steakhouse fries
or
3 1/3 lb (1.5 kg) large starchy potatoes, peeled
vegetable oil[1]

FOR THE 'KETCHUP'

½ cup (110 g) mayonnaise
a few drops of red food dye

If you decide to make French fries from scratch, **start with preparing your potatoes a day ahead.** If you go for the frozen variety, skip to step 4 and begin making your sauces. 1

Peel your potatoes and cut them in long slices, a bit like steak fries. Ideally they should be about 2/3 in (1.5 cm) wide and ½ in (1.2 cm) thick. Put them into a bowl of cold water and gently toss around with your hands to rinse off the excess starch. 2

Drain and move the cut potatoes to a second bowl of clean cold water before putting it in the fridge for 8 hours or overnight. 3

The next day prepare your 'ketchup' & 'mayo'. 4

For your 'ketchup', put your mayonnaise in a bowl and mix with the red food dye until it resembles ketchup. Set aside. 5

For your 'mayo', start by blanching the white tomatoes. Bring a pot of water to a boil. Remove the core from the tomatoes, leaving them whole. Score an X shape at the bottom of each tomato. This is to help with peeling them later. 6

Prepare an ice bath in a bowl and set aside. 7

Place the tomatoes into the boiling water for about 20–30 seconds. Remove and immediately submerge in the ice bath. Once cool enough, peel the skin of the tomatoes off. 8

Cut your tomatoes into smaller pieces and add to a saucepan, along with the remaining 'mayo' ingredients listed on the next page. Bring to a boil then turn down to a simmer. Stir the uncovered mixture frequently until it has reduced by half, for about 30–40 minutes. 9

Use an immersion blender or regular blender to purée the mixture until smooth. Careful as it will be hot. 10

Ladle the 'mayo' into a fine-mesh strainer set over a bowl and press the mixture through to strain out any solids. 11

If your mixture is still a bit thin at this point, cook it further in a clean saucepan, stirring over medium-low heat until it resembles the consistency of mayonnaise. 12

Set aside and cool. 13

Next, poach your chicken. Add your chicken breasts, in a single layer, in the bottom of a pot and pour in just enough stock to cover the chicken. Add your bay leaves and a pinch of salt. Bring to a boil, cover with a lid and turn down the heat to low. After 10 minutes, check if the chicken is done. It should be opaque all the way through and when the thermometer is inserted through the thickest part of the breast should read 165°F (74°C). 14

With tongs, remove the chicken from the poaching liquid and place on a cutting board to cool. Reserve your poaching liquid as you'll need this later. 15

Cook your onion and spices. In a sauté pan, heat your olive oil and add your diced onion. Cook over medium heat for about 5–7 minutes, until the onions have softened but not browned. 16

Add in the garlic and sauté for another minute. 17

Next add the curry powder, paprika, cloves, cinnamon and stir. Sauté for another 30 seconds or so and remove from the heat. Set aside. 18

Once the chicken has reached room temperature, chop it into small pieces and add to a blender along with your onion and spice mixture, ½ cup + 2 tbs (150 ml) of your chicken poaching liquid, vinegar, honey, Worcestershire sauce and salt. Blend until smooth. Taste for seasoning and set aside. 19

Back to the potatoes. If you're going the frozen route, now's the time to cook them according to the package instructions. Then move to step 28. If you're making them homemade, then move to the next step. 20

Remove the potatoes from the fridge. Rinse and drain them, laying the pieces on a paper-towel lined baking sheet and be sure to dry them extremely well. 21

Heat a large heavy bottomed pot filled about halfway with vegetable oil. Attach a thermometer to the pot so you can monitor the temperature and bring the oil to 300°F (150°C).[2] 22

FOR THE 'MAYO'

- 1 ¾ lb (800 g) white tomatoes
- ¼ cup (60 ml) water
- 1/3 cup (66 g) granulated sugar
- ¼ cup + 2 tbs (90 ml) white vinegar
- ½ tsp (1.5 g) onion powder
- ¼ tsp (a big pinch) garlic powder
- scant tsp (3 g) kosher salt
- 1/16 tsp (a small pinch) celery salt
- 1/16 tsp (a small pinch) mustard powder
- 1/8 tsp (a pinch) freshly ground black pepper
- 1 clove, whole

FOR THE CHICKEN FILLING

2 boneless, skinless chicken breasts (1 lb or ½ kg)
2 bay leaves
kosher salt
4 cups (950 ml) chicken stock
2 tbs (30 ml) olive oil
1 cup (130 g) yellow onion, diced
2 garlic cloves, chopped
3 tbs (18 g) curry powder
2 tbs (14 g) sweet paprika
¼ tsp (a big pinch) ground cloves
½ tsp (1.5 g) ground cinnamon
2 tbs (30 ml) apple cider vinegar
2 tbs (30 ml) honey
2 tsp (10 ml) Worcestershire sauce
1 tsp (3 g) kosher salt

Gently place your potatoes into the oil and stir once or twice with a spider or slotted spoon so they don't stick together, this should take about 5 minutes. Do this in batches so you don't overcrowd the pot or cause the oil to drop too low in temperature. 23

When you remove your fries, place them in one layer on a wire rack set over a baking tray, allowing the excess oil to drip off. Repeat with the remaining potatoes until all have been fried once. 24

Bring your pot of oil up to 375–380°F (190–193°C). 25

Fry again for about 3–4 minutes per batch, until fries are golden brown and crispy. Be sure to stir once or twice. 26

With a spider or slotted spoon, remove the fries from the oil and drain slightly before placing them into a large metal bowl. Immediately season with salt and toss to coat. 27

Time to assemble! Immediately after frying, fill a meat/marinade syringe with your chicken purée and inject a small amount into the center of each French fry. We recommend doing this from the bottom or short end of the potato and filling along the whole length of the fry, being cautious not to overfill. Repeat with all French fries and plate with your white ketchup and red mayonnaise. 28

1 You will be deep frying, so be sure to have a large bottle of neutral flavored oil with a high smoking temperature. This includes e.g. sunflower, corn, peanut, etc.
2 The first fry is at a lower temperature so that you can first cook your potatoes without getting too much color.

I'M NOT THE
PERSON YOU

Goodbye Chicken

GOODBYE CHICKEN

BABKA CHICKEN SALAD SANDWICHES

Just as bidding farewell can elicit conflicting emotions, this recipe brings together the familiar with the uncanny. Sweet babka meets salty chicken salad. As you savor each slice, allow the layers of tender dough and flavorfully adorned chicken to bring your taste buds on a journey while simultaneously evoking a sense of nostalgia and longing.

Sometimes a dry and somewhat stale baked good is what you want, for sentimental reasons. But, however fondly Julia remembers the babkas she used to find hidden in the back of her Nana's freezer, in this book we opted for a fluffy, buttery favorite of ours: the babka from Breads Bakery in NYC. We've tweaked the recipe to work with our desired flavors and filling. The dough makes 4 babkas so feel free to include the more traditional Nutella spread with chopped dark chocolate in some of them if you desire.

BREAKABLE
I HATE YOU

Makes 4 Babkas

FOR THE DOUGH
¾ cup (170 ml) whole milk
1 oz (30 g) fresh yeast[1]
2 ¼ cups (325 g) bread flour, sifted
2 ¼ cups (325 g) pastry flour, sifted
2 large eggs, at room temperature
½ cup (100 g) granulated sugar
½ tsp (2.5 ml) vanilla extract
¼ tsp (a big pinch) kosher salt
8 ½ tbs (120 g) butter, at room temperature, cut into cubes

FOR THE BABKA FILLING
3 red onions, diced
1 tbs (15 ml) olive oil
2 tbs (28 g) butter
½ tsp (1.5 g) kosher salt
1 tsp (3 g) cinnamon
1 tsp (3 g) ground ginger
¼ cup (40 g) dates, finely chopped
heaping ⅓ cup (60 g) finely chopped green olives
1 tbs (15 ml) pomegranate molasses

FOR THE SYRUP
7 oz (210 ml) water
5 sprigs fresh thyme
½ cup (100 g) granulated sugar
¼ tsp (a big pinch) kosher salt
extra flaky salt for finishing

FOR THE CHICKEN SALAD
1 whole roasted chicken, shredded[2]
½ cup (110 g) mayonnaise
3 tbs (50 g) Dijon mustard
2 tbs (30 ml) white wine vinegar
½ cup (25 g) parsley, roughly chopped
½ cup (65 g) red onion, finely chopped
½ cup (60 g) celery, finely chopped
kosher salt and freshly ground black pepper to taste

FOR THE SANDWICH GARNISHES
chopped almonds
pomegranate seeds
arugula

1.
Start with the babka dough.[3]
Into the bowl of a stand mixer fitted with a dough hook, break up the yeast into small pieces using your fingertips. Add the milk and start whisking, by hand, to help combine them. The yeast should begin to dissolve into the milk.

2.
Add the flour, eggs, sugar, vanilla, salt and half of the butter. Turn on the stand mixer at a very slow speed to prevent the flour from flying everywhere, and mix for about 2 minutes.

3.
Increase the speed to medium and mix for another 5 minutes. Scrape down the sides of the bowl every once in a while, to be sure everything is getting incorporated. It won't be smooth at this point.

4.
Again, change the mixer speed back to low and, one cube at a time, add in the rest of the butter. You only want to add the next piece once the previous one has been incorporated into the dough. Turn off the mixer. You'll notice the consistency of the dough will have changed at this point, looking more glossy, elastic and smooth.

5.
Remove the dough from the bowl onto the countertop, which needs to be lightly dusted with bread flour.

6.
Knead the dough until smooth, forming a ball. Then shape it into a rectangle about 10 × 6 in (25.5 × 15 cm). Tightly wrap it with plastic wrap and put in the refrigerator for a minimum of 2 hours or ideally overnight.

7.
The next day, start by preparing your babka filling. In a small saucepan or sauté pan, heat the olive oil and butter until melted, over medium-low heat.

8.
Add onions and cook slowly, stirring occasionally for about 15–20 minutes until softened but not browned.

9.
Add salt, cinnamon, ground ginger and stir, allowing the spices to lightly toast for about 30 seconds.

10.
Turn off the heat and add your chopped dates, olives and pomegranate molasses. Stir to combine and set aside.

11.
Start preparing your loaf pans by coating them lightly with vegetable oil or nonstick baking spray.[4] Again, lightly dust your countertop and a rolling pin with some bread flour and transfer your dough to the work surface.

12.
Roll the dough in a rectangular shape measuring (minimum) 36 × 9 in (91.5 × 23 cm), with the long side facing you. If for some reason the dough springs back while you're rolling it, don't stress, just lightly cover it with a towel or plastic wrap and allow it to rest for about 5 minutes before continuing to roll it out.

13.
Once your dough is at the correct size and shape, use an offset spatula to spread the onion mixture evenly on the surface of the dough, all the way to the edges.

14.
For this next step the idea is to essentially **roll your dough** into a log from the side closest to you (the longer side). The process is similar to making cinnamon rolls. It helps if you start at one corner using your fingertips to roll the dough into a *tight coil*. You don't want any gaps between the dough and the filling. When your log is formed you should notice a spiral shape has formed at each end.

15.
Next lift up the log, with each hand on opposite ends and gently stretch it apart to about 48–50 in (122–127 cm) in length.

1 If you live in a place where fresh yeast is hard to come by in the regular supermarket, we recommend picking some up from your friendly local pizzeria.
2 As always, our Backup Plan Chicken has your back here. See page 64
3 This recipe makes enough for 4 loaves. They are best baked in a 8 ½ × 4 ½ in (21 × 11 cm) loaf pan. Ideally you have 2 pans, and can then bake 2 at a time.
4 Since we only have 2 loaf pans at home, we usually cut the dough in half after it has rested overnight in the fridge. We then place the other half of the dough back into the fridge (covered with plastic wrap) until we're ready to bake the other 2 loaves. This usually happens the next day because we can't get enough of them but, theoretically should last for 2–3 days. If you do half the mixture, be sure to adjust the size measurements for rolling them out 18 × 9 in (46 × 23 cm).
5 The slices will certainly be smaller than regular sandwich bread so we serve 2–3 sandwiches per person.

HOW TO BABKA

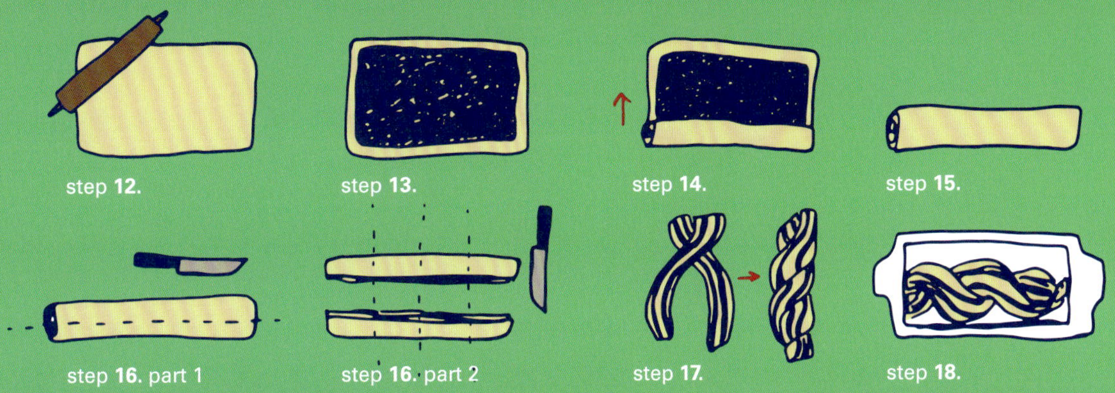

16.
Cut the whole roll in half *lengthwise*, from one end to the other, with a serrated knife. This will leave you with two very long halves. Then cut these both *crosswise* into 4 even pieces, leaving you with 4 pairs.

17.
Starting with 1 of the 4 pairs, place them side-by-side with the cut-side facing up. Lift 1 on top of the other, creating an X shape. Twist the two halves around each other, always keeping the layered cut-sides facing upward. It helps to occasionally, gently pull the pieces lengthwise as you wrap them around one another, so you get a nice, even braided look.

18.
Place the babka in one of your loaf pans and repeat this process with the remaining pairs, giving you 4 babkas in total.

19.
Cover the pans with a kitchen towel and place them in a warm environment (we often use our oven with the light turned on) for about 2–2 ½ hours until the babkas have doubled in size.

20.
While you're waiting, make the sugar syrup. In a small saucepan combine the sugar, water, three of your thyme sprigs and a pinch of salt. Bring to a boil and reduce to a simmer for about 3 minutes. Turn off the heat and allow the syrup to cool to room temperature. Once cooled you can remove the thyme sprigs.

21.
Once your babkas are done proofing, preheat your (empty) oven to 350°F (180°C). Bake in the middle of the oven for about 25–30 minutes until golden brown all over.

22.
When done baking, remove the babkas from the oven and immediately use a pastry brush to coat the loaves *generously* with your thyme-flavored sugar syrup. Sprinkle the warm syrup-covered babkas with the leaves from your 2 remaining thyme sprigs and a bit of flaky salt. Allow to cool completely before removing from the loaf pans.

23.
While the babkas are cooling, **make your chicken salad.** In a mixing bowl, use your hands to shred the whole chicken into bite-sized pieces, discarding the skin and bones.

24.
Add all the remaining chicken salad ingredients into that bowl.

25.
Stir everything to combine and taste to check for seasoning.

26.
Finally, build your sandwiches. With the babkas now at room temperature, remove them from the baking pans and slice.[5] Taking a slice, add a scoopful of the chicken salad, sprinkle this with a few pomegranate seeds, chopped almonds and arugula leaves and top with a second slice of babka.

The collaborative works of artists Gabriele Edlbauer and Julia S. Goodman celebrate the messiness of narratives, embrace emotional ambiguities, empathize with material polyphonies and baffle with culinary delusions. Infused with humor and rarely visually subdued, Edlbauer & Goodman's installations, paintings, sculptures and photographs dynamically weave threads from popular culture, art history, and their everyday experiences. Consequently, they twist, exaggerate and intertwine these elements to construct work-inherent logics which leak uncannily into their surroundings. While their often-excessive installations are as generous as they are mouthwatering, the devil always lies in the details.

Gabriele Edlbauer (AUT) received her diploma from the Academy of Fine Arts in Vienna in 2012 and holds a BFA from the Royal Institute of Art Stockholm, 2011. Julia S. Goodman (USA) received her diploma from the Academy of Fine Arts in Vienna in 2020 and holds a BFA from New York University, 2009. They both live and work in Vienna, Austria.

Our artistic collaborators Albin Bergström, Anna Schachinger, Charlotte Gash and Lennart Schweder; Anna Paul, Alexander Jackson Wyatt, Maruša Sagadin and Miriam Stoney for the many brain-picking sessions about book making; Gregor Anreiter and Philipp Lossau for helping to illuminate our sets; Noële Ody for the Covid cooking madness and driving across borders; Anna Hugo and Yves Michele Sass for responding to our messages in the best way possible; Hugo Vallarta, Laura Hinrichsmeyer, Lennart Schweder, Salvatore Viviano and Stefan Wirnsperger for guiding us with your taste buds; Simon Mraz for your Paprika Hendl and tireless support; all of our patient friends who we have bothered endlessly these past years with questions, excitement, ideas and complaints about this project, especially Florian Regl and Vika Prokopaviciute for your eyes, ears, honesty and encouragement.

This publication was inspired by so many fabulous cooks, places, books and dishes. Here are a few that we kept coming back to along the way: Julia's Grandma Shirley's and Nana Trudy's recipe cards; Alison Roman, Rick Martinez, Thomas Keller & Breads Bakery's flavor profiles, tying techniques, yeast support and proportions; Florian Böhm & Annahita Kamali's Cookbook Book, Dalí's Les Diners De Gala & Plachutta's Classics of Viennese Cuisine to mention a few now thoroughly bookmarked publications on our shelf; finally, and especially, the queen of the Engagement Chicken: Ina Garten.

p. 16
We're Too Entangled Chicken
Engobe painting on pasta bowls: Anna Schachinger

p. 22
I'm a Smoker Chicken
Models: Julian Ernst, Yein Lee

p. 28
You've Changed Chicken
Model: Joan Goodman
Location: Provided by Bob & Joan Goodman
Handwriting: Joan Goodman

p. 34
Let's Just Be Friends Chicken
Models: Charlotte Gash, Susi Schmid
T-shirt courtesy of: Philipp Fleischmann

p. 40
I Want to Move in Chicken
Set in collaboration with: Albin Bergström

p. 46
Let's Take Things Slow Chicken
Models: Andrea Kopranovic, Siggi Sekira
Location: Groteskensaal, Lower Belvedere, Vienna
Production & hand-holding: Andrea Kopranovic

p. 52
I Left the Church Chicken
Model: Noële Ody
Location: Villa Decius Krakow

p. 56
I've Had a Change of Heart Chicken
Model: Isa Schieche
Location: Provided by Philipp Fleischmann

p. 64
You Were Our Backup Plan Chicken
Set in collaboration with: Charlotte Gash
Models: Hyeji Nam, Lukas Gritzner, Nour Shantout, Victoria Dejaco

p. 70
I'm Very Sick Chicken
Model: Katharina Höglinger

p. 76
I Love You Chicken
Models: Hugo Vallarta, Stefan Wirnsperger

p. 82
I Froze My Eggs Chicken
Model: Charlotte Gash
Costume: Charlotte Gash
Location: Provided by Sophie Tappeiner
Ice cream consultant: Noële Ody

p. 88
Let's Be Friends with Benefits Chicken
Location: Kunstraum L201

p. 94
I Hate You Chicken
Models: Southampton seagulls
Transportation: Bob & Joan Goodman

p. 100
Meet My Parents Chicken
Models: Salvatore Viviano, Simon Mraz
Makeup: Charlotte Gash
Accessories: Danielle Pamp
Location: Provided by Sophie Tappeiner

p. 106
Give Me a Second Chance Chicken
Sandwich wrapping paper: Lennart Schweder
Drawing elements in page design: Lennart Schweder
Models: Miriam Stoney, Philipp Lossau
Guard dog: Siggi

p. 112
I'm Not the Person You Think I Am Chicken
Model: Thomas Brandstätter
Location: Café Weingartner, Vienna

p. 120
Goodbye Chicken
Location: Bob & Joan Goodman's driveway
Cardboard boxes courtesy of: Jordan Feil
Yeast courtesy of: La Parmigiana, Southampton

Concept and Editors
Gabriele Edlbauer
Julia S. Goodman

Cover
Julia S. Goodman

All Photography, Artwork and Recipes (unless otherwise noted)
Gabriele Edlbauer
Julia S. Goodman

Typesetting
Laura Catania

Photo Retouching
Giovanni Galilei & Studio

Copy Editing and Proofreading
Jennifer Cunningham
Miriam Stoney

Production
Druckerei Kettler, Bönen

Published by
Verlag Kettler, Dortmund
www.verlag-kettler.de

500 copies printed in Germany

ISBN 978-3-98741-119-9

VERLAG KETTLER

Bildrecht

mit Unterstützung von Kultur ober österreich

Stadt Wien

Federal Ministry
Republic of Austria
Arts, Culture,
Civil Service and Sport

Federal Ministry
Republic of Austria
European and International
Affairs

Stiftung Stark
für Gegenwartskunst

59 ML = 1/4 CUP
79 ML = 1/3 CUP
118 ML = 1/2 CUP
237 ML = 1 CUP

0.63 ML = 1/8 TSP
1.25 ML = 1/4 TSP
2.5 ML = 1/2 TSP
3.75 ML = 3/4 TSP
5 ML = 1 TSP
15 ML = 1 TBSP

2.54 CM = 1 INCH

0°C = 32°F
60°C = 320°F
90°C = 375°F